— Stories Of The —

WORLD'S GREATEST
SPEAKERS

VOL II

VISIONARY AUTHOR: DR. SHAWN FAIR

This book is intended to provide personal growth strategies that will assist the reader in their journey. This book is not intended to provide financial, emotional health, or legal advice. Please seek appropriate counsel for financial, emotional health, or legal matters.

TABLE OF CONTENTS

FOREWORD
VISIONARY AUTHOR: DR. SHAWN FAIR

"There is no greater agony than bearing an untold story inside you."
—Maya Angelou

Everyone has a story, a narrative uniquely their own, shaped by their experiences and journey. As someone who has been privileged to connect with countless individuals from every walk of life, I've witnessed firsthand the undeniable power of these stories. From sitting across the table with Fortune 500 executives to sharing moments with those who have faced unimaginable adversity, one truth remains constant: our stories are our power.

Over the years, I have come to understand that behind every smile, every handshake, and every success lies a story. It's a story that, when shared, has the power to inspire, to heal, and to transform. Unfortunately, not everyone is given the opportunity or the platform to share their story. Sometimes, we are silenced by the weight of our past, societal expectations, or the barriers that exist within our communities. But when we find the courage to share, we create a ripple effect that touches the lives of others in ways we may never fully comprehend.

The stories contained within *"Stories of the World's Greatest Speakers Volume II"* are more than just words on a page. They are testimonies of resilience, determination, and triumph. Each speaker, from diverse backgrounds and experiences, has faced their own set of challenges, yet they have risen above them to become beacons of hope and inspiration. Their stories remind us that no matter where we come from, we all have the potential to rise, to lead, and to make an impact.

In this volume, you will meet eleven extraordinary individuals who have turned their pain into purpose, their challenges into opportunities, and their setbacks into comebacks. These inspirational stories are sure to touch your heart and soul. One author shares the profound transformation as a speaker who turned the sting of rejection into a flourishing career that now serves as a source of encouragement for many.

Another speaker takes us on an incredible journey from the humble beginnings of church hymns to the bright lights of global stages, where faith and passion intersect to create a legacy of influence. One chapter offers a raw and powerful narrative of breaking through societal and cultural expectations to redefine leadership on one's own terms, proving that true power knows no boundaries. There is also a chapter that highlights the remarkable journey of previously incarcerated returning citizens who not only reclaimed their lives but now dedicated themselves to inspiring others who are walking the path of reintegration.

These stories are meant to be more than just read - they are meant to be felt, resonating within the hearts of those traveling similar paths or facing their own trials. They prove that our greatest challenges can become our greatest victories, offering hope and inspiration to all who read them.

As the founder of the Leadership Experience Tour, the #1 platform for speakers in the United States, I've had the honor of witnessing how these powerful stories come to life on stage. Now, through this anthology, these stories will reach even further, touching readers worldwide and continuing to inspire long after the final page is turned.

The contributing authors in this volume have embraced their authentic voice, offering us a gift: a deeper understanding of the human spirit's resilience. They remind us that we all have a story worth telling, and by sharing it, we empower not only ourselves but also those who need to hear it most.

You matter. Your story matters. And just as these remarkable individuals have done, I encourage you to share your truth with the world. Your words have the power to change lives, to inspire action, and to leave a legacy. By sharing your story, whether as a speaker or an author, you not only empower yourself but also those who need to hear it most. The world is waiting to hear from you.

Visionary Author: Dr. Shawn Fair
Global Keynote Speaker | Leadership Trainer | Consultant
CEO, Fair Consulting Group | Founder, Leadership Experience Tour
Visionary, LET Presents Stories of the World's Greatest Speakers Volume 2

Chapter One

A GLOBAL VOICE: HARNESSING MULTICULTURAL ROOTS IN PUBLIC SPEAKING

SASKIA CHRISTIAN

From Nursery Rhymes to Global Stages: The Early Years

My unconventional journey into public speaking took me through diverse cultures and vibrant experiences. Growing up in four different countries shaped my perspective and communication style. Little did I know that this multicultural foundation would be the stepping stone for my extraordinary career as a professional speaker.

From a young age, I was mesmerized by the power of words. My love for public speaking was sparked at the tender age of five when I would listen to my dad's eloquent speeches on agricultural development. His recordings would always start with the sound of mooing cattle, a quirky introduction that left a lasting impression on me. I was in awe of his command over language and ability to engage his audience, solidifying his position as a thought leader.

Following the family tradition, I started showing signs of public speaking talent when, at six years old, I was selected to recite nursery rhymes on the local radio station. "What will poor Robin do then, poor thing?"— my favorite line from the 16th-century nursery rhyme "The North Wind Doth Blow." My adorable facial expressions and hand gestures accompanied those lines, commanding attention in every room.

My passion for public speaking grew substantially during my formative high school years. I was chosen to participate in elocution competitions on behalf of my school team. These early experiences revealed to me the power of effective communication. However, I soon realized I needed more than merely reciting speeches and relying on written notes to foster a deep connection with my audience.

Navigating Cultural Currents: A Multicultural Journey

As I journeyed through various countries and continents, I discovered the significance of tailoring my speaking style to connect with diverse audiences. Initially, my British cultural background and formal tone shaped my approach. However, I soon realized the value of embracing a more contemporary American style to engage a broader range of listeners. This transformation went beyond mere adjustments in my speaking style; it entailed a complete shift in my approach to public speaking, enabling me to convey my message and resonate with a broader audience effectively.

My multicultural upbringing had a profound impact on my perspective and communication style. Growing up in four different countries exposed me to diverse cultures, traditions, and ways of thinking. This experience broadened my understanding of the world and allowed me to appreciate the richness and complexity of different perspectives.

Through my experiences, I cultivated a unique ability to empathize with people of diverse backgrounds and adapt my communication style to connect with them effectively. I honed my skills in recognizing and respecting cultural nuances, fostering trust, and establishing meaningful connections across cultures. My multicultural upbringing fostered open-mindedness and a genuine curiosity to embrace new ideas. This mindset allowed me to engage in thoughtful discussions, challenge my own assumptions, and gain a deeper understanding of diverse viewpoints, enlightening myself and my audience.

Throughout my corporate career as a process engineer, I faced countless challenges. Balancing work and personal life while constantly seeking validation drained me. But amidst the chaos, my speeches became my sanctuary. They illuminated my path, guiding me through pain and uncertainty. Sharing my message of resilience and perseverance, rooted in my own struggles, became the foundation of my content. It struck a chord with audiences who, like me, yearned for inspiration and empowerment.

Rising Above: The Power of Resilience in Corporate Struggles

One pivotal moment in my speaking evolution came when I attended an intensive speaker training program led by the author and Founder of Epiphany's Institute Platform for Purpose, my first anthology cohort. Under the mentorship of esteemed figures in corporate training and journalism, I learned the art of crafting impactful speeches and delivering them confidently and authentically.

My speaking career culminated during the highly anticipated No. 1 US Speaking Tour, The Leadership Experience Tour, hosted by the renowned Shawn Fair. With my newfound mastery of energy control for resilience boosts, I delivered an unscripted, compelling speech that captivated the minds of my listeners. My ability to connect authentically while sharing my personal journey of growth inspired and motivated the 1,000-plus in-person and virtual audience.

My speech at the Leadership Experience Tour marked a significant milestone in my speaking career. It was a testament to years of hard work, dedication, perseverance, and the relentless pursuit of excellence in refining my craft. My speech content no longer merely reflected my current experiences but instead embodied who I was as a person, my resilience brand, and the profound impact I envisioned making in the lives of others.

Another critical component was positioning myself as a thought leader in the speaking and coaching industry. I shared invaluable insights and knowledge online, leveraging platforms like LinkedIn to route my "Tap into Your Resilience Power" newsletter, which garnered over

400 subscribers in a year. This effort strengthened my credibility and attracted speaking opportunities even from the least likely places.

Understanding the power of resilience was also crucial. I developed techniques to maintain a positive outlook and stay motivated despite adversity. This mindset shift allowed me to control my stage fright and deliver successful speeches.

Cultivating emotional intelligence helped me connect with my audience on a deeper level. I fostered healthy relationships and effective communication by understanding and managing my emotions. This skill enhanced my relatability and rapport with my audience, making my speeches more impactful.

Engaging and connecting with my audience was vital. I built a support network of like-minded individuals on a journey of self-discovery and professional development. Sharing experiences and learning from others inspired and motivated me long after my speaking engagements ended.

By applying the power of professional brand enhancement, I stood out as an Executive Trainer and Life Coaching Consultant. This visibility was crucial for my speaking success and helped me build resilience, enabling me to thrive in adversity.

The Turning Point: From Engineer to Inspirational Speaker

One pivotal aspect of my resilience-building and speaker career enhancement was leveraging my creation—a Professional Guide to Developing a Winning Signature Talk Framework. This guide focuses on knowing your target audience, planning your opening, mastering non-verbal communication, and speaking purposefully. By practicing storytelling and leveraging past wins, I refined my speaking skills to connect deeply with my audience.

Knowing your audience is crucial. I researched my target audience's attributes, asking questions like "Who are they? Where do they hang out on the weekend? Where do they visit for morning coffee?" This understanding helped me tailor my speeches to resonate with them.

Another critical element was confidently planning my opening. Using the STAR Method (Situation, Task, Action, Result) helped me prepare for presentations and rehearse answers to crucial questions. Mastering nonverbal communication, such as eye contact and gestures, also significantly engaged my audience.

Speaking with purpose made my words impactful. Providing concise answers during Q&A sessions and demonstrating my knowledge and skills enhanced my credibility. Flexibility and storytelling competency added versatility to my speeches, making them more engaging.

Practicing storytelling was essential. Crafting stories from the audience's perspective and delivering them with eye contact, varied tone, and pitch helped make my speeches more relatable and impactful. Rehearsing in front of a mirror ensured my non-verbal cues aligned with my speech.

Here is my Exceptional Speaker Development Checklist to Master Three (3) Foundational Strategies for Becoming a Competent Professional Speaker:

Strategy 1: Professional Speaker Brand Power Enhancement Kit

A. Harnessing Personal Brand and Influential Power:

- Recognize and leverage your value proposition to fuel your professional speaking career.
- Amplify strengths, cultivate credibility, and foster trust among stakeholders.
- Enhance your brand by adopting a confident identity and showing resilience.

B. Building Brand Visibility for Success:
- Develop a strong reputation in your field by sharing valuable content and collaborating with industry experts.
- Position yourself as a thought leader and resilience expert to attract a more significant following.
- Embrace authenticity, maintain consistency and showcase expertise.

C. Steps to Enhance Brand Visibility and Resilience:
1. Embrace Authenticity:
   - Align your brand with your true self to provide a strong sense of identity and purpose.
2. Maintain Consistency:
   - Ensure consistency across all touchpoints, including online presence, communication style, and visual identity.
3. Showcase Thought Leadership:
   - Share insights and knowledge to position yourself as a credible expert.
4. Understand Resilience:
   - Develop a resilient mindset, manage stress, and stay motivated in adversity.
5. Cultivate Emotional Intelligence:
   - Manage emotions, build empathy, and connect deeply with your audience.
6. Enhance Personal Brand:
   - Use resilience and emotional intelligence to stand out and build trust.
7. Engage and Build Support Networks:
   - Foster genuine connections and build a supportive community.

Strategy 2: Speaking Skillset Refinement Methodology

A. Developing a Winning Signature Talk Framework:
- Know your target audience by researching their attributes and preferences.

- Plan your opening with confidence using the STAR Method (Situation, Task, Action, Result).

  Situation: Describe the context within which you performed a task or faced a challenge at work. For example, you might have been working on a project or addressing a specific problem.

  Task: Explain your responsibilities or what you were tasked with. This could include your role in the project or the specific challenges you needed to overcome.

  Action: Describe the specific actions you took to address the task. This should highlight your contribution and the steps you took to resolve the issue or complete the task.

  Result: Share the outcomes of your actions. Focus on what you accomplished and any tangible benefits, such as increased efficiency, successful project completion, or positive feedback from clients or stakeholders.

B. Mastering Non-Verbal Communication:
   - Practice strong eye contact and confident gestures.
   - Maintain clarity and speak with a purpose to make your words impactful.

C. Leveraging Storytelling and Flexibility:

   1. Know the Takeaway:
      - Focus on the main message you want your audience to remember.
   2. Craft Stories from the Audience's Perspective:
      - Anticipate their questions and expectations to connect better.
   3. Practice Delivery:
      - Rehearse in front of a mirror and seek feedback to improve.
   4. Be Vocal About Self-Improvement:
      - Share your learning journey and demonstrate continuous improvement.
   5. Draw from Past Wins:
      - Use past successes to build confidence and credibility.

D. Enhancing Engagement and Follow-Up:
 1. Listen Actively:
    • Show engagement and understanding through verbal affirmations.
 2. Inquire Intelligently:
    • Ask insightful questions to reflect your interest and understanding.
 3. Follow Up Effectively:
    • Send follow-up emails to thank your audience and reinforce connections.
 4. Celebrate Achievements:
    • Celebrate milestones and reflect on performance to boost self-confidence.

Strategy 3: Fusion of Diverse Cultural Backgrounds into Signature Speech Framework

A. Impact of Multicultural Upbringing:
    • Embrace cultural diversity to enrich your communication style and broaden your perspective.
    • Develop empathy and adapt communication to connect with various backgrounds.

B. Building Trust and Establishing Connections:
 1. Recognize Cultural Nuances:
    • Respect and adapt to cultural differences to build trust.
 2. Approach Conversations with Curiosity:
    • Embrace open-mindedness and willingness to learn from others.
 3. Engage in Thoughtful Discussions:
    • Challenge assumptions and foster a deeper understanding of different viewpoints.

C. Preparing for a Major Speech:
 1. The Wake-Up Call:
    • Use your journey to hone communication skills and understand audience needs.

2. Power of Energy Control:
   - Manage energy levels to deliver impactful speeches and avoid burnout.
3. The "Aha" Moment:
   - Share personal stories and insights to add authenticity and credibility.

Action Plan:

1. Reflect on your personal brand and identify areas for enhancement.
2. Develop a signature talk framework and practice non-verbal communication.
3. Embrace your multicultural background to connect with diverse audiences.

Following these strategies allows you to become a competent and impactful professional speaker. Embrace authenticity, refine your speaking skills, and leverage your unique cultural background to inspire and uplift your audience.

Leadership Experience Tour (LET) Speech:

Unleashing the Power Within: Mastering Energy Control for Unprecedented Success

Ladies and gentlemen, distinguished guests, and fellow procrastinators, good morning/afternoon/evening!

Today, I stand before you to introduce a revolutionary idea that will transform the way you approach your daily lives. It's time to unleash the power within and master energy control for unprecedented success. Are you ready for this energy control extravaganza experience?

But before we dive in, let's kick off this journey with a little game. I want everyone to stand up, stretch those limbs, and shake their bodies like they're at the most significant Caribbean festival! Feel the rhythm and beat, and let your energy levels reach new heights. Shake off those day blues and embrace the power of joy and laughter!

Now that we're all energized and ready to conquer the world, let me share what life looked like for me before I discovered the secret sauce to winning. Like many busy wives, I constantly raced against the clock, especially during the holiday season. But let me tell you something, fellow busy wives: your honey-do list is cute, but it does not make you productive! Even your husbands' stress levels are skyrocketing as they struggle to meet your demands. It's time to say, "Fire bun them to-do lists like the Jamaicans say!

As an engineer in the corporate world, I was caught up in the hustle and bustle of life, at the mercy of the pager. I was constantly on the run but with nothing to show for it. I used to wear my packed schedule like a badge of honor, proudly proclaiming, "Look at me; I'm so busy!" But deep down, I was overwhelmed and burnt out.

Then, one day, I had my "aha" moment. I discovered the true power of energy control and prioritization overtime management, and it transformed my engineering career and saved my life. You see, controlling your energy levels builds up your resilience muscles. Time is finite, but our energy can be renewed and replenished. It's about understanding our energy levels and knowing when to push forward and take a step back. It's about prioritizing tasks based on their impact and aligning them with our energy peaks. Embrace your natural energy rhythm and use it to your advantage. This mindset shift allowed me to become more productive, focused, and, most importantly, resilient.

You see, the Boost*Thru* resilience boost platform is not just another self-help or motivational program. It's a way of life—a philosophy that empowers individuals to pursue self-care, take control of their energy, prioritize what truly matters, and build unwavering resilience. We often neglect ourselves in the pursuit of productivity, leading to burnout and plummeting energy levels. It's time to change that. Take breaks, eat nutritious meals, get enough sleep, and engage in activities that bring you joy. Remember, you can't pour from an empty coconut shell.

Imagine a platform that offers life-saving tools, techniques, and strategies to help you trade toxic stress, anxiety, depression, and burnout for resilience, joy, and thriving. You get to take your power back! Boost*Thru* offers workshops, corporate conference training programs, online self-paced e-courses, personalized coaching, and physical resources designed to support your journey toward a more resilient and fulfilling life without sacrificing your well-being.

So, my fellow energy enthusiasts, I invite each of you to join me on this transformative journey with Boost*Thru*. Together, let's embrace the power of energy control and build a world where resilience is not just a buzzword but a healthy way of life.

Thank you, and may the abundant energy source be with you! I am Saskia Christian, the Founder of Boost*Thru*™ life coaching service and your Trauma Healing and Resilience Life Coach.

Let's empower you to break free from the shackles of time management and unlock your maximum potential. Don't you deserve it?

Thank you, my friends!

Closing Remarks

Overall, my experience on that phenomenal LET tour stage has equipped me to connect with my listening audience, inspire action, and convey the transformative power of energy control and resilience. My journey leading up to that LET tour speech added authenticity and credibility to my message, making me a compelling and relatable motivational speaker.

Self-Reflection Exercise

To emerge as a branded, powerful, and authentic professional speaker, reflect on the following questions:

1. What makes a great speaker?
   Guidance: Consider the qualities that make a speaker engaging, such as authenticity, confidence, and the ability to connect with the audience.

2. What have you done to develop your speaking skills?
   Guidance: Reflect on the steps you've taken to refine your speaking skills, such as attending training programs, practicing storytelling, and seeking feedback.

3. Suggestions for becoming a great speaker:
   Guidance: Identify tips and tools that have helped you in your journey, such as knowing your audience, mastering non-verbal communication, and leveraging your personal brand.

4. Personal Experiences:
   Guidance: Recall specific events or circumstances that led you to speak and how those experiences have shaped your journey.

5. Past Speeches and Presentations:
   Guidance: Reflect on your past speeches and presentations, noting the lessons learned and how they have contributed to your speaking growth.

By fusing the strategies of professional brand enhancement, speaking skill refinement, and embracing a multicultural perspective, you can emerge as a powerful and authentic professional speaker. Embrace your unique voice, confidently share your stories, and inspire others with your journey.

SASKIA CHRISTIAN

Saskia Christian is an accomplished Trauma and Global Resilience Expert with a remarkable background. With 17 years of corporate visionary engineering leadership experience, she excelled as a technical leader. However, her path took an unexpected turn, leading her to become a renowned Training Executive, Trauma Healing and Resilience Coaching Consultant, Speaker, and Founder of BoostThru.

Saskia's expertise extends beyond her corporate success. She is a prolific author, with her book "Mindset Mastery" showcasing her ability to unlock mind power. She has authored e-courses on Seasonal Resiliency and co-authored five anthologies, including an International Bestseller. Notably, her story about her father's disappearance in "Resilient A.F: Stories of Resilience" gained recognition at The 2024 Oscar's gift lounge.

Saskia is a Brainz Magazine Executive Contributor and has received CREA and GSFE Kindness global awards. As a Resilience Trailblazer, her work significantly impacts the lives of professionals in distress. Her purpose-driven comebacks inspire hope and resilience, making a profound difference in the lives of those she works with.

Website: www.boostthru.com/contact
Email: saskiac@boostthru.com
LinkedIn: http://linkedin.com/in/saskia-christian
Facebook: https://www.facebook.com/profile.
             php?id=100088422974533&mibextid=LQQJ4d
Instagram: https://www.instagram.com/boostthru

Chapter Two

UNLOCKING POTENTIAL: GUIDING GROWTH FROM ASPIRATION TO ACHIEVEMENT:

FROM COMBAT TO CONSULTANCY: CHERYL MONROE'S JOURNEY

CHERYL MONROE

The early morning mist clung to the Georgia landscape as Cheryl Monroe walked the familiar streets of her hometown, Atlanta, Georgia. Born into modest beginnings, Cheryl's life seemed predetermined to follow a path of limitations. But she was determined to forge a different path, not just for herself but for her son. At sixteen, faced with the reality of teenage motherhood, Cheryl made a pivotal decision at nineteen that would alter the course of her life: she enlisted in the United States Army.

In 1991, Cheryl began her military journey as an Ammunition Specialist (55B). Basic training was grueling, pushing her to her physical and mental limits. The military environment was predominantly male, and Cheryl quickly realized that she would have to work twice as hard to gain the same recognition and respect as her male counterparts. The stereotypes and biases she encountered only fueled her determination to succeed.

Cheryl's resilience and exceptional performance did not go unnoticed. She rapidly climbed the ranks, traveled globally, and held multiple leadership positions. Each role presented new challenges and opportunities for growth.

Throughout her 28-year military career, Cheryl deployed into combat six times. Each deployment was a testament to her strength and leadership under pressure. Her commitment to her fellow soldiers and her ability to navigate the complexities of logistics in war zones earned her numerous commendations and respect from her peers.

On December 3, 2017, Cheryl made history by becoming the first African American female in the ammunition field to be promoted to Chief Warrant Officer Five (CW5). Her induction into the U.S. Army Women's Foundation Hall of Fame on March 11, 2020, was a crowning achievement, recognizing her trailblazing career and significant contributions to the military.

By the time she retired on December 31, 2020, Cheryl had served as the Senior Logistics Warrant Officer in the Office of the Deputy Chief of Staff, G4 at the Pentagon. In this role, she also served as the Program Manager for the Department of Defense National Level Ammunition Capability (NLAC) and the U.S. Military Representative for the North Atlantic Treaty Organization Ammunition Interoperability Working Group, collaborating with representatives from 28 nations.

Cheryl's transition from combat to consultancy was seamless, driven by her desire to continue making a difference. She founded CK Management and Consultant Group (https://ckmacg.com), a consultancy dedicated to assisting small businesses in navigating the complex arena of government contracting. Cheryl's firsthand experience in operational contracts, logistics, supply chain management, and project management gave her a unique perspective and skill set.

CK Management and Consultant Group's mission is clear: to empower small businesses to excel in government contracting. Cheryl understood the intricacies of this space, from the certification processes to compliance requirements. Her consultancy offered end-to-end support, ensuring that businesses were not only certified but also met all regulatory standards.

One of CK Management and Consultant Group's key areas of focus is set-aside contracts, reserved for businesses owned by veterans, women, and other minority groups. Cheryl's consultancy guided clients through the certification process for various programs, such as the Women-Owned Small Business (WOSB), Service-Disabled Veteran-Owned Small Business (SDVOSB), Disadvantaged Business Enterprise, Minority Business Enterprise, and other relevant certifications based on the state requirements.

Unlocking Potential Through Government Contracts: Doing business with the government can unlock tremendous potential for small business owners, enabling them to scale their operations, increase revenue, and achieve long-term growth. Government contracts provide a stable and reliable source of income, allowing businesses to invest in their capabilities, hire additional staff, and expand their market reach. The certification programs and set-aside contracts offer unique opportunities for underrepresented groups to compete on a level playing field and secure significant contracts that can transform their businesses.

Navigating the Government Contracting Landscape: *A Guide for Small Businesses:* Entering the world of government contracting can unlock significant potential for small businesses, providing opportunities for growth, stability, and increased revenue. However, it requires careful planning, thorough preparation, and an understanding of the benefits and challenges involved. This chapter offers a guide for small businesses looking to do business with the government, outlining what they should consider, some available resources, and the pros and cons of government contracting.

CK Management and Consultant Group offers the following advice for small businesses considering entering the government contracting space:

What to Consider Before Entering the Government Contracting Space

1. Understand Your Readiness:
   - **Assess Capabilities:** Ensure your business has the necessary capabilities, capacity, and expertise to meet the demands of government contracts.
   - **Financial Stability:** Government contracts often involve delayed payments; ensure your business can maintain cash flow during these periods between 30-120 days.
2. Compliance and Regulatory Requirements:
   - **Certifications:** Determine which certifications (e.g., WOSB, SDVOSB, HUBZone) are relevant to your business and pursue them.
   - **Regulatory Compliance:** Familiarize yourself with federal, state, and local regulations that govern government contracts.
   - **Remain Compliant:** Regularly review and update your compliance practices to stay aligned with evolving regulations
3. Market Research:
   - **Identify Opportunities:** Research potential contracting opportunities within your industry and understand the needs of various government agencies.
   - **Competitive Analysis:** Analyze the competitive landscape to identify your unique selling propositions and potential competitors.
4. Proposal Preparation:
   - **Detailed Proposals:** Develop the ability to craft comprehensive, compliant, and compelling proposals tailored to specific government solicitations.
   - **Understanding RFPs, RFQs, and RFIs:** Learn how to interpret and respond to Requests for Proposals (RFPs), Requests for Quotes (RFQs), and Requests for Information (RFIs).

5. Building Relationships:
   - **Networking:** Establish connections with procurement officers, prime contractors, and other businesses in the government contracting ecosystem.
   - **Industry Events:** Attend industry days, conferences, and networking events to gain insights and build relationships.
   - **Leverage Partnerships:** Collaborate with larger firms as a subcontractor to gain experience and build a history

Resources Available to Small Businesses

1. Small Business Administration (SBA):
   - The SBA offers various resources, including certification programs, training, and counseling services to help small businesses navigate government contracting.
2. Procurement Technical Assistance Centers (PTACs):
   - PTACs provide free or low-cost assistance to businesses seeking to compete for government contracts. They offer guidance on bidding, compliance, and market research.
3. Small Business Development Centers (SBDC)
   - SBDCs provide counseling and training to small businesses including working with SBA to develop and provide informational tools to support business start-ups and existing business expansion.
4. SCORE Business Mentoring
   - SCORE mentors offer area-specific advice at no cost (financing, human resources, business planning) via email, telephone, and video.
5. Veterans Business Outreach Center (VBOC) Program
   - VBOC program offers resources to veterans, service members, and military spouses who are interested in starting or growing a small business.
6. Women's Business Centers
   - They provide free, to low-cost counseling and training and focus on women who want to start, grow, and expand their small businesses.

7. Federal Contracting Websites:
    - **SAM.gov:** The System for Award Management (SAM) is the primary database for vendors doing business with the federal government.
    - Serves as a portal for federal procurement opportunities, where businesses can find and respond to federal contract solicitations.
8. Mentor-Protégé Programs:
    - Programs like the SBA's All Small Mentor-Protégé Program help small businesses gain capacity and win government contracts by partnering with more experienced companies.
9. Government Agencies:
    - Many agencies offer resources and support for small businesses, including the Department of Defense (DoD), General Services Administration (GSA), and Department of Veterans Affairs (VA).
10. State Contracting Websites (varies by state):
    - Serves as a portal for state procurement opportunities, where businesses can find and respond to state and local contract solicitations.
    - You can also sign up for a free account on Bidnet Direct to search for opportunities in your state.

Pros and Cons of Doing Business with the Government
Pros:

1. Stable and Reliable Revenue:
    - Government contracts provide a consistent and reliable source of income, helping businesses stabilize cash flow and plan for long-term growth.
2. Large Market Opportunities:
    - The government is one of the largest buyers of goods and services, offering a vast market with diverse opportunities across various industries.
3. Certification Benefits:
    - Certifications such as WOSB, SDVOSB, and HUBZone can provide a competitive advantage and access to set-aside contracts reserved for small businesses.

4. Long-Term Contracts:
   - Government contracts often span multiple years, providing long-term revenue streams and opportunities for business expansion.
5. Credibility and Prestige:
   - Successfully securing government contracts can enhance a business's credibility and reputation, making it easier to attract other clients and partners.

Cons:

1. Complex and Lengthy Processes:
   - The government contracting process is often complex, involving extensive documentation, strict compliance requirements, and lengthy timelines.
2. Intense Competition:
   - The competitive nature of government contracting can be challenging, with many businesses vying for the same opportunities.
3. Payment Delays:
   - Government payments can be delayed, which may strain a small business's cash flow and financial stability.
4. Regulatory Burden:
   - Meeting regulatory and compliance requirements can be time-consuming and costly, requiring dedicated resources and expertise.
5. Risk of Contract Termination:
   - Government contracts can be terminated for convenience, which may disrupt business operations and financial projections.

Practical Advice for Small Businesses Entering Government Contracting

1. Start Small:
   - Begin with smaller contracts or subcontracting opportunities to build experience and credibility in the government contracting space.

2. Invest in Training:
   - Continuously educate yourself and your team on government contracting best practices, compliance, and proposal writing.
3. Leverage Technology:
   - Utilize technology and software solutions to streamline proposal development, compliance tracking, and project management.
4. Build a Strong Team:
   - Assemble a team with diverse skills and expertise in areas such as finance, compliance, proposal writing, and project management.
5. Seek Expert Guidance:
   - Consider collaborating with consultants or advisors who specialize in government contracting to navigate the complexities and increase your chances of success.
6. Monitor and Adapt:
   - Continuously monitor your performance on government contracts and be prepared to adapt your strategies based on feedback and changing requirements.

Entering the government contracting space can be a transformative journey for small businesses, unlocking new opportunities for growth and success. By carefully considering the challenges and leveraging available resources, small businesses can position themselves to thrive in this competitive and rewarding market.

As a small business owner who has successfully secured contracts at both the state and federal levels, CK Management and Consultant Group understands that the road to government contracting is not always easy. The process can be daunting, and the challenges are real, but the rewards can be significant. Cheryl's journey from military service to consultancy has provided her with invaluable insights into what it takes to succeed in this space.

Cheryl emphasizes the importance of patience and perseverance. "The path to securing government contracts is filled with hurdles, but each one is an opportunity to gain experience and grow," she says. "Stay committed, be adaptable, and never stop seeking ways to improve your processes and offerings."

Steps to Navigating Government Contracting with CK Management and Consultant Group:

1. **Initial Consultation and Assessment:**
   - The team begins with an in-depth consultation to understand the client's business, goals, and readiness for government contracting.
   - A thorough assessment identifies strengths, weaknesses, and potential opportunities.
2. **Certification Guidance:**
   - The firm provides detailed guidance on obtaining necessary certifications, including WOSB, SDVOSB, and others.
   - Assistance with application preparation and submission to ensure compliance with all requirements.
3. **Compliance and Regulatory Support:**
   - CK Management and Consultant Group ensures that clients meet all federal, state, and local regulatory requirements.
   - Regular compliance audits and updates to keep clients aligned with evolving regulations.
4. **Market Research and Analysis:**
   - Detailed market research identifies potential government contracting opportunities relevant to the client's industry.
   - Analysis of competitive landscape and identification of unique selling propositions.
5. **Proposal Development and Bid Preparation:**
   - The team assists in crafting compelling and compliant proposals tailored to each government solicitation.

- Training on the bidding process, including tips for responding to Requests for Proposals (RFPs) and Requests for Quotes (RFQs).

6. **Strategic Planning and Business Development:**
   - Development of a strategic plan that aligns with the client's long-term goals.
   - Business development support to build relationships with key government agencies and prime contractors.

7. **Training and Workshops:**
   - Regular training sessions and workshops on topics such as government contracting basics, compliance, capability statement and effective proposal writing.
   - Customized training programs to address specific client needs.

8. **Post-Award Support:**
   - Ongoing support after contract award to ensure successful execution and compliance.
   - Assistance with contract modifications, renewals, and performance reporting.

9. **Networking and Partnerships:**
   - Facilitation of networking opportunities with other small businesses, government agencies, and industry partners.
   - Encouragement of partnerships and collaborations to strengthen client capabilities.

10. **Continuous Improvement and Feedback:**
    - Regular review and feedback sessions to assess progress and make necessary adjustments.
    - Encouragement of a culture of continuous improvement and innovation.

As Cheryl Monroe's story demonstrates, unlocking potential and guiding growth from aspiration to achievement is not only possible but also immensely rewarding. With the right guidance, determination, and strategic planning, small businesses can navigate the complexities of government contracting and achieve remarkable success.

In addition to her consultancy work, Cheryl served as a trusted technical adviser for federal contracts and opportunities. She performed as the technical solutions lead for internal and external solution development, including proposals, Requests for Proposals (RFPs), Requests for Quotes (RFQs), and Requests for Information (RFIs). Cheryl's role involved putting together comprehensive solutions across multiple towers, creating supporting literature, diagrams, write-ups, responses, and presentations. Her ability to articulate complex technical solutions and demonstrate their value to potential clients was a key factor in securing contracts and driving business growth.

CK Management and Consultant Group's impact is far-reaching. Cheryl's clients ranged from start-ups to Fortune 500 companies, each benefiting from her strategic insights and deep understanding of public sector business dynamics. Her consultancy not only helped businesses secure contracts but also provided strategic planning, leadership development, and operational efficiency services.

Cheryl's passion for helping small businesses thrive in the government sector extended beyond her consultancy. She became a sought-after speaker, sharing her insights and experiences on diverse topics. Her speaking engagements covered a wide range of subjects, including:

- **Leadership:** Cheryl shared her journey of overcoming challenges and rising to leadership positions in the military, offering valuable lessons on leading with integrity, resilience, and vision. She has been honored with the prestigious 2024 United Nations Global Women Foundation Leadership Award and the 2024 Presidential Lifetime Achievement Award.
- **Logistics and Supply Chain Management:** Drawing from her extensive global experience, Cheryl is certified as a Demonstrated Master Logistician, Project Management Professional, and Knowledge Management Integrator

Processor who provides expert advice on optimizing logistics and supply chain processes, crucial for success in both military and civilian sectors.

- **Navigating Government Contracting:** As a certified Contractor Officer Representative and Business consultant, she demystified the complexities of government contracting, offering practical tips and strategies for securing and managing government contracts.
- **Women Empowerment:** Cheryl inspired women to break barriers and achieve their full potential, emphasizing the importance of confidence, determination, and support networks.
- **Military-Related Topics:** She spoke about her military career, sharing stories of her deployments and the lessons learned from serving in combat zones.
- **Motivational Topics:** Cheryl's motivational talks focused on overcoming adversity, setting and achieving goals, and unlocking one's potential through perseverance and hard work.

Her consultancy's success is measured not just in financial terms but in the real-world impact on the businesses she supported. Entrepreneurs who once struggled to navigate the complexities of government contracting found themselves winning bids and growing their companies. Cheryl's guidance turned their aspirations into achievements, unlocking their potential and setting them on a path to success.

Cheryl's journey from a teenage mother to a history-making military leader and successful business consultant is a testament to the power of resilience, determination, and strategic thinking. She had faced numerous obstacles, both in the male-dominated military and in the competitive business world, yet she emerged victorious. Her favorite quote, "The journey is a tapestry of achievements, woven together by the threads of resilience and perseverance," perfectly encapsulates her approach to life and business. Through CK Management and Consultant Group, Cheryl continues to provide a lifeline to small businesses, guiding them through the complex world of government procurement and positioning them for enduring success.

As Cheryl looks towards the future, she remains committed to her mission of empowerment. Her story is not just about personal achievement but about creating a legacy of support and success for others. She had unlocked her potential and now guiding countless others to do the same, proving that with the right guidance and determination, anything is possible.

As you consider venturing into the world of government contracting, remember that preparation, persistence, and leveraging the right resources are key to unlocking your business's potential. The journey may be challenging, but the rewards can be transformative, providing stability, growth opportunities, and enhanced credibility.

CK Management and Consultant Group are here to help you every step of the way. Whether you need assistance with certifications, compliance, proposal development, or strategic planning, our team of experts is dedicated to empowering small businesses like yours to excel in the government sector.

Take action today:

- **Schedule a Consultation:** Schedule an initial consultation and assess your readiness for government contracting https://calendly.com/cmonroe-7/government-contracting-advice
- **Attend a Workshop:** Join one of our upcoming training sessions or workshops to gain valuable insights and skills.
- **Connect with a Mentor:** Leverage the Mentor-Protégé Program to partner with experienced businesses and enhance your capabilities.

Visit our website at https://ckmacg.com or email us at admin@ckmacg.com to learn more about how we can support your journey.

Unlock your business's potential and achieve growth from aspiration to achievement. The opportunities are there – seize them with confidence and determination. Your success story in government contracting starts now.

CW5(R) CHERYL MONROE

CW5(R) Cheryl Monroe is a distinguished business strategist, author, dynamic speaker, and decorated military veteran. As the CEO of CK Management and Consultant Group, she leads a global transformative consultancy with a singular focus: empowering small businesses to excel in the complex arena of government contracting.

With three decades of military experience, her passion for mentorship, speaking, and training is not just a part of her work; it's a part of who she is. Her dedication to empowering businesses with the knowledge and strategies needed to thrive is not just palpable; it's infectious. She identifies opportunities for growth, helping clients streamline processes and maximize their potential in securing government contracts.

Her thought leadership extends to various prominent publications, including CEO Weekly, Shoutout ATL, K.I.S.H. Magazine, and Tap in Magazine. Cheryl's expertise has also been showcased on Onstage Plus TV, further cementing her status as a leading voice in her industry.

Website: https://ckmacg.com
Email: Email: cmonroe@ckmacg.com
Facebook: https://www.facebook.com/cheryl.monroe.96
Instagram: https://www.instagram.com/ckmacg_20/
LinkedIn: https://www.linkedin.com/in/cheryl-monroe/

Chapter Three

FINDING HARMONY MY BALANCING ACT NAVIGATING THE DUAL ROLES OF CAREGIVER AND PHYSICIAN LEADER

KIMBERLY BATTLE MILLER, MD, MS, MBA

I often wonder: Are caregivers born with servant hearts, developed through life's experiences, or created out of necessity when thrust into the fire? In truth, I know it is probably a combination of all three. Personally, I believe I was born to serve others. This realization came at about five years of age when I declared that I wanted to be a doctor. As improbable as it sounds for a five-year-old to make such a decision, it might explain why my siblings called me "special" and why I never felt like I fit into most crowds. The Bible explained it best to me when, at eleven, I read John 17:14: "Believers are in the world but not of the world" (paraphrased). I realized then that feeling displaced in this world was not a bad thing; it was by God's design.

Born the fifth child of Joe and Blanche Battle, it seemed I frequently carried the responsibility of directing my four older siblings back to the road of righteousness. They called it tattle-telling; I called it looking out for their best interest. As we grew into young adulthood, my siblings lovingly renamed me "the Baby Boss." After becoming a physician, I may have become more intrusive in how my siblings and parents lived. My directives expanded beyond encouraging them to do the right thing but also to live healthily, to promote longevity so we could grow old together. I credit the years of navigating my stubborn siblings as the training ground where I honed my skills as a physician in an executive leadership position.

As our parents grew older, all heads turned towards me to care for them. My dad developed dementia at 75 years old after a mild stroke with seizure and over a 5 year period, progression of his dementia resulted in him becoming dependent with his physical and financial care. At 80 years of age, dad suffered a second stroke leaving him totally dependent for all his care. We had a family care conference which ended in my mother and 4 siblings insisting that because I was a physician, I should move my father to my home. I remember the day because precisely three weeks after experiencing the bliss of becoming empty nesters, I had to ask my husband to give up his recently acquired "man cave" to convert it to a hospital room. Because I am married to a man with a servant's heart, he manifested his love for me by offering his blessing and support without hesitation, agreeing to share this responsibility. While I would never change the decision to give my father a safe and comforting home, where my medical knowledge allowed me to establish a plan of care that offered respect, dignity, and minimal hospitalizations, I wish I had received a course in caregiving without jeopardizing my own physical and mental health. Especially since being a caregiver was added to an already busy life of being a wife, a mother of three sons, a full-time physician leader, a business owner, and active in the community and church.

I failed to mention I was already the caregiver to my godmother Gladys, who was a vibrant hospice volunteer for 14 years until she injured her hip at 81-years-old. I cared for her in her assisted living apartment, until she suffered a stroke on her 94th birthday, after which, I had to move her to my home. Our empty nest became a full quiver. I appreciate that my dad and Mama Gladys made caring for them easy. They rarely pushed back during care, adapted to changes well, and often said, "Thank you, Baby". It was no fault of either of them that their irregular sleep habits, unsteady gait with multiple near-falls, and successful falls created a PTSD-like response in my husband and me. Nor was it their fault or desire when I fell down the stairs, twice trying to prevent my godmother from falling, and when I developed stress-

Visionary Author: Dr. Shawn Fair

induced prediabetes and hypertension from not recognizing that I was not superwoman.

My physician told me I had three months to get my hemoglobin A1C and blood pressure down. I realized then that what I thought was a balanced life was indeed a rollercoaster ride of unpredictability, physical strain, stress, and a little anger and resentment because no one showed up longer than 30 minutes to help. I realized that if I continued neglecting myself, I could die or, worse, become debilitated, needing a caregiver myself. If I did not become intentional about self-care, my dad, godmother, husband, sons, new granddaughter, mother, siblings, staff, and ministry members would soon be mourning my loss and scrambling to fill the void my debility or death would create.

It wasn't that I hadn't seen this happen to many of my patients' caregivers, nor that I needed to gain knowledge of what self-care entailed and the consequences of not purposefully including yourself in the caregiving schedule. I already told you I was born a caregiver, so I had a lifetime of developing my skills. But I didn't tell you that I also literally wrote the book, *A Guide for Caregivers to Navigate the Rewards and Challenges of Caring for a Loved One*. So, I was at a crossroads of practicing what I preached or preparing my eulogy for the preacher. I chose the former.

I looked at my home and work schedules and made minor changes that I knew would greatly impact my immediate and long-term physical, mental, and financial health. I also knew it would guard my marital health, which was a priority because my husband and mother's support was the only constant in this rollercoaster caregiving life. I chose to live my Dr. Kim Today business motto: "Health and Wellness, you can achieve it!" and "Don't seek balance, seek harmony."

I made five simple changes that I could do, for free, from home in between caregiving duties:

1. **Healthy Eating:** I stopped eating fast foods and skipping meals and started eating simple, healthy meals that could be prepared in 20 minutes or less. The internet is full of ideas from people who have walked in the caregiver's shoes of chaos. I took

advantage of what I learned during the pandemic – everything can be ordered online and delivered to your home in the blink of an eye. As a result, not only did my hemoglobin A1C lower, getting me off the pre-diabetic list, and my blood pressure normalize, but my husband, dad, and godmother also reaped similar benefits (decreased medication, improved digestion, no more constipation, better sleep, improved immune health).

2. **Daily Walks:** I started walking 30 minutes daily at home or on the block. A patient who was healthy at 103 years old told me if I wanted to live a long, healthy life, drink a cup of black coffee every morning, and walk back and forth between the rooms in my house for 30 minutes praying blessings over myself, my family, my household, and those things that are important to me. This one action had the greatest impact because I began to lose my stress weight, regained my calm mindset and demeanor, and reestablished my connection with God, my family, and my friends. After I finish praying over the important desires of my heart, I call up a family member or friend, making the 30 minutes a treat rather than a chore.

3. **Prioritized Sleep:** I stopped working into the wee hours of the morning and vowed to turn off my computer by 10:00 pm regardless of how many emails were unchecked or which deadline loomed. This simple change increased my sleep from four hours a night to six to seven hours a night. Now, instead of waking up with a sleep-deprived headache, I wake refreshed and get more done in the two hours before caregiving starts than I ever did working through the night.

4. **Asking for Help:** I learned to ask for help and not assume people should know I needed help working full-time and caring for two debilitated seniors in my home. I stopped feeling resentment because my siblings dropped by for 5-15 minutes, took a selfie with Dad as proof they "showed up," then headed right out the door without a care or offer to donate their time or money to the cause of caring for OUR father. I made a list of what help I needed physically and financially, then called a family meeting. Even though only half of my "needs" list was fulfilled, it was enough to feel as if the caregiving load was now being shared. My sister who lives locally agreed to cook and

deliver healthy meals to my home every other week. Reducing both our grocery bill and the time needed to prepare meals. My sister living out-of-state and my mother, committed to splitting the cost of hiring a part-time private duty caregiver. My mother also adopted shopping for necessary supplies. We joke about her becoming an "Errand Girl" at 80 years of age. My brothers, a carpenter and plumber, agreed to respond to requests for repairs and remodeling expeditiously and at no cost. The greatest benefit of forming this caregiving team was that it lessened the number of jabs my husband took at my family for insisting we move our dad to my house and then disappearing into their own lives.

5. **Gratitude Journaling:** Lastly, I resumed gratitude journaling nightly (I wrote the book on this, too – *A Caregiver's Weekly Gratitude Journal*). I keep a copy of the gratitude journal I published on my nightstand, and every night, I review my day and jot down three highlights. What did we do or what was said that brought out a smile or laughter from my dad or godmother? What was something positive that happened at work? What was something my husband did or said that reminded me why I married him 30 years ago?

By intentionally maintaining these five small changes and giving myself grace if I missed a day doing any of them, I created harmony in my life. I regained my joy, health, and peace. Best of all, the last three years of caregiving have been done cheerfully and without injury to me or my precious seniors.

I share my story not because I think I'm a saint; however, I hope I'm paying it forward, and this will indeed help me get into heaven. I share my story because before I lived it, I wrote about it, I told my patients about it, yet I didn't put it into practice, and it almost cost me my health and, potentially, my life. I know I am not the only one who has lived such a story or is currently living this story. By the way, since November of last year, I'm also caring for a cousin who has dementia at 72 years of age and is progressing rapidly. I've moved her from state to state because it's become difficult for other family members to care for her, and now, she, too, is under my umbrella of care. But because my husband and I continued to practice what I preached for years, we were able to incorporate my cousin into our web of love without causing additional burdens or risks to ourselves.

I share what I have learned in books, prescribed for my patients' caregivers, trained leaders and my mentees to practice, and lived personally, which has gotten us all to a place of harmony and good health. Whether you were born to be a caregiver, developed into a caregiver, or were forced into being a caregiver, have hope and know that there is a way to do it well and minimize the risk to your physical, mental, and financial health.

Ok, I tried to avoid letting my physician's brain encroach on telling my story, but I think I would be remiss not to add a few additional proven strategies and mindset shifts that have significantly improved my caregiving journey and can help you, too.

Before I proceed, I must share this important **disclaimer:** The information provided in this chapter is based on my personal experiences and professional insights. However, I am not making any medical recommendations. It is essential that you consult your healthcare provider before implementing any of the ideas discussed here. Your healthcare provider can give you guidance tailored to your unique situation.

That being said, caregivers should consider:

Prioritizing Your Health: As a caregiver, it is crucial not to neglect your physical health. Ensure you do not miss appointments with your healthcare provider, comply with their recommendations, and integrate your health routine into your caregiving schedule. Taking care of yourself is vital to sustaining your ability to care for others.

Embracing Flexibility and Patience: Caregiving requires a significant amount of flexibility and patience. While creating a structured routine reduces stress by providing stability and predictability in your daily caregiving tasks, be aware that there will be days when everything goes wrong—appointments get canceled, medications are forgotten, and tempers flare. On those days, remind yourself that it's okay to have setbacks and that each day is a new opportunity to start fresh. Learn to adapt to the changes and challenges that come your way with a positive mindset. My favorite quote at home and at work is: "The Only Constant Is Change." Once you grab this concept, you will view change not as a barrier or something being done to you. You will recognize it for what it is… "change," and you will adapt accordingly.

Building a Support Network: One of the most crucial aspects of caregiving is having a reliable support network. This includes not only family and friends but also professional support such as counselors, support groups, and medical professionals. Don't hesitate to reach out and build a team around you that can provide emotional support, practical help, and professional advice. Isolation can lead to burnout, so make it a priority to stay connected with others. A quick phone call to laugh, cry, grumble, celebrate, or confide is an inexpensive way to release stress.

Practicing Self-Compassion: As caregivers, we often hold ourselves to incredibly high standards. It's essential to practice self-compassion and recognize that you are doing the best you can in a challenging situation. Acknowledge your efforts, celebrate small victories, and forgive yourself for any perceived shortcomings. Remember, taking care of yourself is not a luxury; it is a necessity. Give yourself grace for what goes undone, celebrate the small wins such as: "We both took a shower today," and learn to laugh a lot.

Exploring Respite Care Options: Respite care is a valuable resource for caregivers. It provides temporary relief, allowing you to rest and recharge. Respite can be provided in your home or at a facility. Look into local respite care services, which can range from a few hours to several days. This break can significantly reduce stress and prevent burnout, giving you the strength to continue your caregiving duties effectively. I list respite resources in my book. You can also contact your insurance case manager or hospital or clinic social worker to inquire about available respite services.

Continuing Education and Skill Development: Caregiving is a dynamic role that requires continuous learning. Stay informed about the latest developments in caregiving practices, medical advancements, and support resources. The internet is a valuable resource to educate yourself on your loved one's disease and what to expect. Attend workshops, webinars, and training sessions to enhance your skills and knowledge, as well as meet kindred spirits who understand your journey. The more equipped you are with information, the better you can care for your loved ones and yourself.

One chapter limits my ability to share all the thoughts swirling in my mind, and it surely does not afford me the opportunity to share all the antics of my dad and godmother, who, even in their advanced dementia states, have occasional moments of quick sarcastic wit.

So, I leave you with this final thought:

If you can relate to this story or know someone who is living a similar story, please visit my website for caregiver resources or reach out to me so that I can share what I have learned in books, prescribed for my patients' caregivers, trained leaders and my mentees to practice, and lived personally, that has gotten us all to a place of harmony and good health.

Whether you were born to be a caregiver, developed into a caregiver, or were forced into being a caregiver, have hope and know that there is a way to do it well and minimize the risk to your physical, mental, and financial health.

I invite you to explore the following resources and opportunities to further support your caregiving journey:

1. **Read My Book:** Dive deeper into the strategies and insights shared in my book, *A Guide for Caregivers to Navigate the Rewards and Challenges of Caring for a Loved One.* This comprehensive guide offers practical advice, personal anecdotes, and expert tips to help you thrive as a caregiver.

2. **Attend My Seminars and Workshops:** Join me at one of my seminars, workshops, or retreats designed specifically for busy caregivers. These events provide hands-on training, valuable resources, and the opportunity to connect with other caregivers who share similar experiences.

3. **Book Me as a Speaker:** If you are part of an organization, support group, or conference, consider booking me as a speaker. With clinical and experiential expertise, I offer engaging and informative presentations tailored to the needs of caregivers, especially those in leadership roles.

4. **Participate in Webinars and Online Courses:** Access my webinars and online courses from the comfort of your home. These sessions cover various aspects of caregiving, self-care, and balancing professional responsibilities, providing you with the tools and knowledge to succeed.

5. **Connect with My Caregiver Community:** Join my online caregiver community for ongoing support, resources, and encouragement. Share your experiences, ask questions, and learn from others who understand the challenges and rewards of caregiving.

By taking these steps, you can empower yourself to be a more effective caregiver, safeguard your well-being, and create a harmonious life for yourself and your loved ones. Remember, you are not alone on this journey, and there is hope, help, and support available.

Lena Horne said it best: "It's not the load that breaks you down, it's the way you carry it."

KIMBERLY BATTLE MILLER, MD, MS, MBA

Kimberly Battle Miller, MD, MS, MBA has thirty years of experience as a Board-certified Palliative Care & Hospice Medical Director, Pediatric Critical Care Attending, and Integrative Medicine Attending. Currently, she serves as System Medical Director of Palliative Care and Hospice at a 9-hospital medical center, driving program expansion, and overseeing clinical operations. In 2023 she was the recipient of the Presidential Award for COVID-19 Community Service. She is a dedicated wife, mother, grandmother, author, speaker, and respected physician focused on empowering professional women in leadership by providing tools and support for achieving career and personal life balance.

Entrepreneurial ventures:

- H.O.P.E. International: Founder/President/Non-profit health educators in underserved communities.
- Dr. Kim Today LLC: CEO/Health and wellness center for professional women, caregivers, and aspiring entrepreneurs.
- Dr. Kim Today Academy: Founder/CEO/Phlebotomy and nursing assistant training programs.
- United For Health 2020 LLC: Co-founder/CMO/Community-based health education on current health matters.
- Serves as an elected board member of the American Association of Public Health Physicians and a longtime member of Alpha Kappa Alpha Sorority, Inc.

For additional information, contact me at: https://drkimtoday.com/contact-dr-kim-today

www.drkimtoday.com

Website:	www.drkimtoday.com
Email:	drkimtoday@gmail.com
Facebook:	https://www.facebook.com/kimberly.battle.127
	https://www.facebook.com/kbattlemiller
Instagram:	https://www.instagram.com/iamdrkimtoday/
LinkedIn:	https://www.linkedin.com/in/dr-kimberly-battle-miller-md-ms-mba-79b6a666

Chapter Four

FROM CANCER TO COURAGEOUS, A LEADER'S S.U.C.C.E.S.S. JOURNEY TO LIVE!

DR. LISA YVETTE JONES

This chapter serves as a beacon of hope and a practical guide for anyone grappling with the challenges of health crises, the power of leadership, one of the effects of obesity, and living a life of healing and wholeness. My personal journey, marked by a transformative struggle with obesity and a battle with stage 3 cervical cancer with no symptoms and two death sentences, underscores the profound impact my faith and that health can have on one's ability to lead well, look well, live well, and to love well. By sharing my story, I aim to illustrate that overcoming these obstacles is possible, emerging stronger and healthier, and truly leading by example.

The strategies and insights presented in this chapter are not merely theoretical; they are proven methods I employed to reclaim my health and enhance my life, personally and professionally—these Seven S.U.C.C.E.S.S. Strategies—focused on self-care, health awareness, commitment, and mindset shifts—are designed to help individuals Lead, Look, Live, and Love well.

Through this narrative, I hope to empower others to make positive changes, demonstrating that navigating and triumphing over these intertwined challenges with faith, determination, and the right strategies is possible. My life is a testament to the resilience of the human spirit and a call to action for leaders to prioritize their health as a cornerstone of their S.U.C.C.E.S.S.

The year 2009 started like every other year. Each January 1st, I am excited about new beginnings and new opportunities. The immense feeling of hope, renewal, and a fresh restart fuel me to forgive myself for what I did not do the year before and resolve to do it the current year.

In February of 2009, my family and I received what we thought was the worst news ever. Our dear mother, Queenie Victoria Thompson, was rushed to the hospital. She had a mild stroke. As we gathered around her bed, she was cognizant and hopeful that she would overcome that setback. As the leader of our family, a single mother of seven grown children and seven grandchildren, she was determined to bounce back after her setback to do what she loved: spending time with her family, singing for the Lord, and cooking our favorite meals. The doctors also encouraged us that she would do just that, and she did.

After two months in the hospital, many tests, rehabilitation, and much love, prayers, and support from her family, her church, and her neighbors, in April 2009, my mother and my birthday month, our mother was released from the hospital and the rehabilitation center with a clean bill of health and no residual effects of the stroke. God is so good!

After caring for my mother, I gave myself an early birthday gift. You know, ladies, that gift that we give ourselves every year, that yearly appointment that we dread, the one where we are undressed from the bottom down and in stirrups on a cold, hard padded table, and with a very invasive procedure that leaves us most vulnerable, but it is also the appointment that we know that we must keep. Now that is a power nugget right there - keep all medical appointments, particularly that one whether sexually active or not.

That appointment turned into another; I was before two gynecologic oncologists before I knew it. Yes, two cancer specialists. With empathy and concern, I heard these words, "Ms. Jones, you have been diagnosed with stage three Cervical Cancer - Papillary Serous Carcinoma of the cervix. It is high-grade and quite vicious, as you are already in stage 3. Of course, I was in denial. I had a shock wave go across my body, and then I was back to reality within seconds or minutes. Who knew? I certainly had no clue because I had no symptoms or familial history. BTW- I received this news while on my lunch break from work as the surgical team contacted me to confirm my surgery for a diagnosis I knew nothing about. I was still waiting for the results of my biopsy.

I could not understand how that ugliness that they claimed was growing viciously inside of me and that could potentially kill me. How was that possible? My intelligent brain could not comprehend it. There was no precursor for this diagnosis, and let us not forget, I had no symptoms, no irregularities, and no familial history. But was there a precursor?

At the time of my diagnosis, I was every bit of 362 pounds. I looked good, and I felt good. Yes, I looked good because if I did not think and believe it, nobody else would, right? I was divorced one year prior, but I am doing great in my career as a leader with my agency and making great strides in leading successful teams. Nevertheless, I needed more information and a better understanding of the news I received. I did what any intelligent person would do; I began to research and ask a ton of questions. After careful research, I found out those 362 pounds were my warning, my precursor, my danger of cancer.

The Center for Disease Control (https://www.cdc.gov/cancer/risk-factors/obesity.html) (CDC) has studies that reflect that 40% of the cancers in America are related to obesity. Wow! *Disclaimer:* I am not implying that everyone who is obese will have cancer; what I am saying is that science does reflect that there is a cancer/obesity link. In fact, in recent years, the CDC has highlighted the alarming connection between obesity and cancer. Obesity is not just a condition; it is a significant risk factor for various health issues, including cancer.

The CDC identified nine types of cancer that have a strong correlation with obesity in the United States, and five are listed below:

1. Breast Cancer (Postmenopausal)
2. Colorectal Cancer
3. Esophageal Adenocarcinoma
4. Liver Cancer
5. Ovarian Cancer

Obesity affects the body in many ways. For many, receiving a cancer diagnosis linked to obesity is a wake-up call that necessitates life-changing and transformative decisions.

After consulting with the oncologists, I advised them I needed some time. The doctors reminded me that because of the viciousness of the cancer that they diagnosed, I did not have time. They advised that if I did not have the surgery within the next few days, but no later than a week, I would certainly die because once the cancer spread to any major organ, they would not open me up. I insisted that I needed time because I was faced with a storm, and at that moment, I was in duress, and I needed to send out my SOS for healing enforcement.

After both doctors gave me a death sentence, that I would die, I still knew that there was still greatness left in me, and I just could not hear of a death sentence. I left the doctor's office and called on a few key people I knew who knew the words and the worth of prayer. I called Mother Laura Heard. Everyone needs a prayer warrior like Mother Laura Heard in their life. I then called a couple of other prayer warriors, including my now-late ex-husband and my son's father, Anthony Maurice Jones, Sr. Although divorced, we remained great friends and co-parents of our amazing son, Anthony Maurice Jones, II. Because we were still so close when it came to all our son's business. After our separation and divorce, I prayed that God would make me a "Better Woman" and not a "Bitter Woman." A better woman I am indeed!

When I told my ex-husband the news, he was kind and compassionate but quite shocked. He said, "We will get through this as a family, sweetheart." He immediately stood with me and by me during my entire ordeal.

One of the strategies that helped me was knowing my community of support. You must know those who will stand in faith with you when you are facing a storm. I had to do what I would normally do in any storm. I had to get into a shelter, shut out the storm, and shut into God. I had to not only join my faith with their faith, but I had to believe that I was going to come through that storm because I wanted to live, and there was no way in the world that I was going to accept those death appointments at that time. Sure, my good book (Bible) says it is appointed unto man, once to die, but I did not plan to keep that sentence then.

I faced a couple of other dilemmas; I could not tell our mother what I had just found out. Not right away, anyway. She was still in her recovery and doing amazingly well. I could not imagine sharing the news with her and setting her back by taking the news too badly. Our son was accepted into a very prestigious magnet high school, Cranbrook Kingswood, in Bloomfield Hills, MI, as a boarding student on a full scholarship. He was completing the 9th grade, and his finals were the following week, from my diagnosis. If I shared the news with him before he could complete his finals, I risked the chance of him possibly failing and missing out on the fully paid scholarship to attend this school. I could not take that risk. His education meant the world to his daddy and me. Here I was, facing life or death, and I was still putting others before me. I had to in this instance. I am glad that I did. The timing was everything, and I would not change how I planned to share the news with everyone.

The fight to live was on. I had to choose life and living. This was personal. Facing a cancer diagnosis can be overwhelming, but it can also be a powerful catalyst for change. In my case, choosing life meant embarking on a journey of transformation and a true test and testament of my faith. Each day presented a new challenge and opportunity to make decisions that would positively impact my health and well-being.

As a leader, the stress and demands of daily decisions can be immense, often pushing us to the brink of burnout. It is crucial to remember that Leaders' Lives Matter Too.

Leadership comes with its own set of challenges and responsibilities. The constant demands on our time, talent, and resources can leave us feeling drained and overwhelmed, yet empowering and rewarding. However, amidst these pressures, it is essential to prioritize our own health and well-being. As leaders, we often place the needs of others above our own, but self-care is not selfish; it is necessary.

After three days of fasting, praying, and laying before the Lord, on the third day, I heard these words, "You shall live and not die, and this will never return again. And, I have called you into the ministry."

Hallelujah! I began giving God all the glory, honor, and praise that He deserved. I also knew that it was time to shift my mindset to begin living my life on the other side of the diagnosis. Although I respected the doctors for their diagnosis, I fully TRUSTED God for my prognosis. I knew where to draw the line of my faith with the medical team because I needed the assistance of my Chief Physician, my Lord and Savior, Jesus Christ. Of course, God could have miraculously healed me; however, He had chosen another path for me.

On June 29, 2009, I had surgery to remove the cancer. By the way, the doctors were shocked that I was still alive and that the cancer had not spread any further. It was a first for them. Remember, they told me that if I did not have the surgery within a few days or at least a week or so, they would not perform the surgery because of the type of aggressive cancer and that it would have spread to my major organs. If it did spread, it would be unnecessary to open me up because it would be too late. Well, they said that in mid-May. I remind you that the surgery was on June 29, 2009. Look at God! Not only did I surpass the few days to one week or so requirement for surgery, I waited an entire month and a half. God knew what He was doing so that, medically and physically, no one could take credit for what He was doing in and through me.

In 2011, when I reached a turning point, March 23, 2011, became the absolutely worst day of my life and that of my family. Our dear mother made her transition from earth to glory. It was not expected. I was the last person with her the night before. Rest on in glory, dear mother. We love you.

Despite surviving cancer, I was still struggling with obesity, the very condition that had contributed to my illness. I realized that I needed to make a drastic change if I wanted to lead effectively and live a fulfilling life. This decision led to a quest for permanent weight release, not weight loss, but weight release, because whatever is lost can potentially be found. I had no intention of ever finding those pounds again. I have successfully released over 200 pounds, and I am more committed than ever to maintaining my health.

Through my journey, I developed The Seven S.U.C.C.E.S.S. Strategies for Transformation that were crucial to my journey. These strategies can help anyone seeking to improve their health and well-being:

1. Self-care is Not Weak or Selfish; It is Necessary!
   - As leaders, our lives matter, too. Taking time for self-care yields the greatest return on investment. You are worth the effort and attention.
2. Understand the Importance of Your Health Numbers!
   - Understand and know your numbers and other vital statistics. Awareness is crucial because what you do not know can harm you. For instance, hypertension rates are disproportionately high among African Americans, underscoring the importance of regular health check-ups.
     - How much do you weigh/date? _____/_____
     - What is your blood pressure/date?_____/_____
     - What is your cholesterol level/date? _____/_____
     - What is your blood sugar level/date?_____/_____
     - What is your blood type/date? _____/_____
3. Cultivate a Community of Authentic Relationships!
   - Building genuine relationships can empower both others and yourself. Remember, your well-being is as important as that of those you lead and love.

4. Champion Your Own Cause and Commit to Self-Check-Ins!
   - Strive to be the person you look up to. Show others that it is possible to prioritize self-care while leading effectively. Your team is always watching you and taking notice. What a beautiful opportunity to model leadership than starting with leading yourself first. People began to champion and encourage me more as they saw me take the lead in my health and wellness journey, and many began doing the same.
   - Schedule regular check-ins with yourself, just as you would with your team. Use these moments to assess your health, set goals, and plan for your well-being.
   - Be relentless about advocating for your health. You are a partner in your health care.

5. Elevate Your Value and Your Expectations!
   - When you expect that there is more for you, you nurture it, walk in it, and feed it until you are hungry for more. DO NOT waste time.
   - Walk in your greatness and put the world on notice that you are still here, present, and accounted for. Will it be easy? No! But there is no greater joy than leading by the Power of your Example and not by the Example of your Power.

6. Share and Get Excited About Your Transformation!
   - Share your journey with those you love. Your enthusiasm and commitment to self-improvement can inspire and benefit others.

7. Shift Your Mindset and Start Today!
   - A shift or a slight change in perspective can make all the difference. Embrace shifts in your journey and confront the issues weighing you down. Taking care of yourself is about prioritizing your own needs and well-being. You deserve to be at your best.
   - Start now! Make today your January 1st!

In his book "Make Today Count," John Maxwell emphasizes the importance of daily discipline for success. Reflecting on the decisions we make concerning our health, it is vital to identify and practice the necessary disciplines every day.

The journey from Cancer to Courageous, along with fighting obesity to health, is possible. By adopting these Seven-S.U.C.C.E.S.S. strategies and making a daily commitment to our well-being, we can transform our lives as we lead by example. Remember, Leaders' Lives Matter Too. Leader, you matter! Prioritizing our health is not just a personal victory; it's an essential part of effective leadership to Lead well, Look well, Live well, and Love well.

DR. LISA YVETTE JONES

Dr. Lisa Yvette Jones, the Chief Caring Officer of iC.A.R.E. Leadership, LLC. Lisa supports professional leaders to maximize their leadership influence by creating a vocational culture of compassionate caring. And to live out their Self-Care S.U.C.C.E.S.S. while holistically transforming and humanizing the employment experience, head, hands, and heart. Lisa is a John Maxwell Certified Leadership Coach, Teacher, Trainer, Speaker, Les Brown Power Voice Systems Graduate, and Speaker, an International Amazon Best-Selling Author (7X), and an early detection cancer awareness evangelist. Lisa enjoys reading, forever learning, spending quality time with family, and long weekend drives.

Website: LisaYvetteJones.com
Email: LisaYvetteJones@gmail.com
Facebook: https://www.facebook.com/lisa.yvette.jones
Instagram: https://instagram.com/lisayvettejones2:
LinkedIn: LisaYvetteJone1

Chapter Five

THE ADVERSITY: LIFE AFTER CANCER

KIMBERLY L. BYERS

Imagine being told by your mom, "I have cancer, and I'm scared." Fortunately, I didn't hear these words. Instead, my mom said these words to me, "I have cancer; I am going to fight hard and as long as it takes." No one wants to hear about having cancer, let alone having to tell family members of their diagnosis.

Life after the cancer. I was told four times in a row, "I have cancer," by multiple family members in a matter of 1 ½ years. My mom, Valerie, was the first person diagnosed. The ripple effect of hearing the other three was difficult. It was a hard pill to swallow. In my mind, I thought, how is this possible, and why is it affecting my family? To hear these three words was devastating for our family.

When you think about terminal illnesses and how they affect a family, you become afraid. You can't imagine life without your loved one. What does life look like after cancer? What do you do when all your family members have passed away? Do you try to remember what their faces look like and what their voices sound like? Did you tell them you loved them? Did you tell them how much you would miss them? Loss is difficult, no matter what words are said or not said. This is all a part of adversity. You now are faced with the question, "What does life look like after cancer?" Have you thought about that? What would your life look like after a terminal illness diagnosis?

When you think about facing life after cancer, there are some things to consider. In the event of a loss, how do you move from grieving to celebrating the life of your loved one? You may need to redefine yourself when the loss touches your job or is connected to a relationship. What do you do to redefine yourself? Perhaps you will need to take training courses, get a degree in something you are passionate about, or go where you can meet people who enjoy doing the things you enjoy. My family was faced with grief and loss. We chose to preserve the memory of our loved ones by planting memory trees in our yards. Remember that It's important to continue to go to places your loved ones enjoyed while they were living. To remember your loved one, you can write a book or paint a memory and frame it.

As a family, we decided to research the different types of cancer (triple negative breast, colon, rectum, and stomach) plaguing our family members so that we could be educated. Interestingly, no one person had the same cancer diagnosis. Therefore, the treatment and care were not the same. One constant thing was the need to stick together, pray, and ensure we supported one another. Challenging, yes, we all lived in different parts of the U.S.

Our family has a strong bond. Thus, the diagnoses were all rough on us. Technology helped solve some of our distance problems by enabling us to call often, FaceTime, and send messages to say I'm thinking about you today. We brought lots of humor to our talks and videos. It's amazing how laughter can really soothe the soul. The hurt was there, but we still found moments to laugh and poke fun. Telling stories was often a huge part of our loved ones day/night. It was also helpful to keep a journal. We did things like think of the person who was providing care. When the caregiver needed a break, someone would step in to assist. We would be there to talk, ride to the doctor, or sit in the moment. God played an intricate part in how we handled things. We knew that God would not place more on us than we could handle. We were encouraged to know that God would give us the tools to move forward.

Also, it helps to reach out to others who can provide insight into what you are currently dealing with. People like extended family members, mentors, clergy, or a person of trust. These people offer advice, and they will have experiences that resonate with you and help you to feel comfortable confiding in them. This is helpful for multiple reasons. First, it is a safe place with no judgment. You can relax and decompress while talking about your loss. Second, when you speak with someone like a mentor, chances are your mentor's values are similar to yours, and you can have a very informal yet candid conversation about how you are feeling and doing. Third, if you speak with a coach, the coach will provide a more formal set of tools and attach goals to help move you forward.

Hardships will inevitably touch our lives in health, career, relationships, or any other area. Death and loss are examples of things that can happen that could stop us in our tracks. When you lose a loved one, it is not always sudden or planned. It's never wanted. Loss happens to us all. We differ in what we do in life to move forward from the loss.

Adversity is defined as a misfortune or troubling situation. Adversity doesn't necessarily have to be viewed negatively. However, you must work through adversity, or it may harm the essence of your purpose in life. How do you handle adversity? How does it look in your life? How do you get through troubling situations, hardships, or misfortunes? You must remember that you cannot stay in a sunken place. If you don't move, you do not grow, nor can you pursue your purpose in life. Your purpose is waiting for you. Good can come from being in a hard place because being there frequently leads you to your purpose. The key to handling the situation properly is to remember that you cannot stop. Keep moving. As devastating as a cancer diagnosis is, it can lead you and guide you to your purpose, but you must move through the process. Are you ready?

We are all destined for greatness. Do you know what your purpose is? How would you reach your purpose in life? Can you see through the misfortune or the trouble in your life? Imagine, if you will, the possibilities of making it to the other side of adversity. Your loved one passed away, you lost the job you loved, a relationship did not work, or your child is living recklessly. How would your loved one that has gone on feel about you remaining in a stuck place? My belief is our loved ones would not want us to stay dwelling over their passing. We want to reach for better. A better job. A better relationship. A better life. We must continue to have hope. Those no longer here would want us to pray for our families and look toward the future. They would want us to move on and create a fulfilling life. Faith can be the pivotable place in our lives. Without faith, we have nothing. Faith drives our purpose. Yes, life after cancer is possible if you want it.

Being destined for greatness does not mean adversities won't exist, but the hardship is a part of a more excellent plan. God has a plan for every one of us. Adversity is a part of HIS plan. Do you believe that trying situations occur by mistake? They do not and can be a part of God's divine order for our lives. We all will go through tough circumstances. Good, bad, big, or little. We all must face something. It is with adversity that we move, grow, and learn. You will prevail when you can see the light at the end of the tunnel.

Life after the cancer is not just about death. Yes, that is the challenge I focused on; however, adversity can look different at different times in life. It is about everything you could go through in your life to break you. Even more so to stop you from following your purpose. Like the things we did in facing a cancer diagnosis, it's important to remember to stay on the right path; even when it is tough, do not waiver from it. You may pause and stop to breathe but never quit. Giving up cannot become your option. Do not give in. What will you do to get through it?

You're going to have to find methods for silencing the critics. People will be in your ear, telling you how terrible you are. They will say that you're not good enough for the job you seek, you're too short, too tall, too dark to white, too this or too that. At the end of the day, other people's thoughts and opinions should not matter. You cannot let the naysayers get into your head or bring you down. You must know your worth, know you are enough, and deserve all God has for you. Remember, what is for you is for you and no one else. When one door shuts, another door opens. Keep the faith.

There certainly are mental strongholds that come with the challenges that I've been talking about. Mentally, you may not feel like you should do anything. You may feel challenged by your own limited beliefs. For instance, you believe that you cannot change your situation. Perhaps being told your family suffers from a disease like cancer, and you will too. You may think relationships never work out in your family because it's not for you. You may think that good things are available for others, but these things are not for people like you. This list could go on. These thoughts and beliefs are used to stop people from growing and moving past adversity. Whether you were told, saw it growing up, read it in a book, or thought it on your own, do not let your limited beliefs stop you from living life to the fullest. Are you limiting yourself? You may have even heard that bad things happen to bad people. Please understand that good and bad things happen to good and bad people. Nothing is off limits, and we must take the limits off ourselves to grow, learn, and prosper in our purpose.

Let me share some tips with you. These tips will help you navigate life, your purpose, and your adversities.

Tip 1: Embrace changes when they enter your life; learn from them.

Tip 2: Encourage yourself daily with positive affirmations.

Tip 3: Change is not a bad thing; yield to it and look at it from a positive perspective. Use it to your advantage.

Tip 4: Increase your knowledge when faced with an adversity you did not expect; draw strength from it.

Tip 5: Enrich your faith. Scripture helps you to develop and gain understanding in life.

Tip 6: Empower yourself with the knowledge that life is not perfect, but you can live it to the fullest if you believe you can.

These tips will help you to live a more purposeful life and not dwell on the "would of, could of, and should of" in life.

As a coach, speaker, mentor, and author, I am passionate about helping and watching others grow. My prayer is that you find a way to move forward purposefully and without regret. You, too, will have lots to share with others. You have wisdom, life, and great memories to help you progress. Do not let your adversity allow you to miss your opportunity to bless and help someone. Life is too short, and we all need each other to live. Don't let your gifts die with you. Sharing is caring.

I'm Kimberly L. Byers, CEO of ByHers Peace of Mind. Please do not hesitate to contact me with any questions. I'm here to assist you. You can reach me at @iamkimbyers on all social media platforms, my website @www.byherspom.com, email kim@byherspom.com, or text 571-604-5573. Also, look for my book on Amazon: Grief Almost Had, Peace Brought Me Out! 7 Steps From Grief to Peace.

KIMBERLY L. BYERS

Kimberly L. Byers stands as a beacon of resilience and inspiration. As the visionary CEO of ByHers Peace of Mind, LLC, Kimberly's mission transcends coaching; it's a commitment to leading women through the intricate dance of life's challenges and triumphs.

With an illustrious 28-year military career, including multiple deployments across diverse landscapes, Kimberly is not just a speaker; she's a seasoned leader, drawing from a well of experience that has shaped her into the dynamic force she is today. Her journey unfolded amidst profound loss, with a paralyzing car accident threatening her military dreams. Yet, this journey propels her passion for guiding others — not merely to overcome obstacles but to navigate them with purpose and resilience.

Kimberly's transformative journey has graced prestigious stages nationwide, from news/radio interviews to the One Woman: Fearless International Women's Summit and the Leadership Experience Tour at Michigan State University in Detroit, MI.

Website: www.byherspom.com
Email: kim@byherspom.com
Facebook: https://www.facebook.com/IamKimByers
Instagram: @iamkimbyers
LinkedIn: @iamkimbyers

Chapter Six

FROM HYMNS TO THE SPOTLIGHT - THE JOURNEY OF A SPEAKING CAREER

DR. LINDA R. JORDON

Introduction

Becoming a successful speaker often starts with the smallest of steps. For me, it began with a shy, seven-year-old country girl standing nervously before a congregation, clutching a hymnal and singing her heart out. My path was not straightforward; it was filled with challenges, setbacks, and pivotal moments of self-discovery. This chapter delves into the early days of my journey, illustrating how singing in church at the age of seven laid the foundation for my speaking career and highlighting the obstacles I eventually overcame.

Early Beginnings: Singing in Church

My first experience with public performance came from reading scriptures and singing at my local church. The church was a small, close-knit community where everyone knew each other, and Sunday services were a blend of spiritual rejuvenation and social gathering. My parents, active members of the congregation, choir, deacon board, and missionaries encouraged me to participate in the youth choir. Initially, I was hesitant; I was more comfortable hiding behind my mother's skirt than standing in front of an audience. However, the piano player and my older siblings, James and Vanessa, saw something in me that I did not yet see in myself. When you come from a large family, having your older siblings encourage you to be the best is nice.

Challenge of Stage Fright

Stage fright was my first and most significant challenge. Standing in front of the church to sing or read a scripture as a child was terrifying. My knees would shake, my palms would sweat, and my voice would quiver. Being from a large family and being the middle child, I wanted to perform flawlessly. So, the fear of making a mistake or disappointing myself was overwhelming. But each mistake I made was a lesson in resilience. I learned the importance of preparation and practice, understanding that even seasoned performers have moments of doubt.

My older brother, James, with his gentle guidance, taught me to focus on the music and the message rather than the audience. He encouraged me to close my eyes and imagine I was singing directly to God, which helped to calm my nerves. He often told me to sing from the gut, not the nose, as I sometimes did. At that time, I didn't always understand what that meant, but I continued to do my best. Looking back on those experiences has helped me to overcome those fears as an adult.

Building Confidence Through Repetition

Confidence is not something that comes overnight; it is built through repetition and experience. Each Saturday, we would practice for the upcoming Sunday service, and I would try a little harder to build my confidence. At each Sunday service, I sang a little louder, stood straighter, and felt braver, especially when I had to be the lead singer. Having the congregation's support was crucial. They were not just an audience; they were my extended family, cheering me on and celebrating my small victories. This positive reinforcement was instrumental in building my self-esteem and preparing me for the more significant challenges ahead. As I continued to develop as a lead singer, my siblings, cousin Tammy, and two family friends created a singing group. We called ourselves the Inspirational Six and traveled locally to sing at church events and programs. This really helped me to continue to build my confidence, remove some of the fear of stage fright, and strengthen my voice.

Transitioning to Speaking

As I grew older, my involvement in church activities expanded beyond the choir. I began participating in youth group meetings and Bible study sessions, where discussions were an integral part. It was during these discussions that I discovered my love for speaking. I realized that I had a voice that people listened to, and I had ideas worth sharing. My younger sister, Janice, encouraged me to join her in managing the youth group, where we were responsible for all youth activities, such as the youth choir, youth Sunday School, and more. We would also support the youth by singing with them during the fourth Sunday services. We also trained the youth members to speak in the church by focusing on reading scriptures and learning to say a prayer.

The Challenge of Finding My Voice

Finding my voice was a journey in itself. Initially, I mimicked the speaking styles of those I admired, such as my mother, Eliza Russell, and my Aunt Annie Pearl Russell. However, I quickly learned that I needed to change my mindset and realize that authenticity was key. People could tell when I was trying to be someone I was not. My older brother always told me to just be myself, focus, and sing from the gut. I needed to find my unique voice that resonated with my personality and experiences. This process involved a lot of self-reflection and trial and error. I experimented with different tones, pacing, and storytelling techniques until I found a natural and engaging style.

Overcoming Criticism and Self-Doubt

One of the biggest challenges I faced was self-doubt. Transitioning from singing to speaking was not always smooth. Sometimes, I questioned my abilities and whether I was truly cut out for this path. Imposter syndrome often crept in, making me feel like I didn't belong on stage as a speaker. Criticism and self-doubt were constant companions on my journey. Not everyone appreciated my speaking style or agreed with my viewpoints. Sometimes, negative feedback made me question my abilities and path. However, I learned to view criticism as an opportunity for growth rather than a setback. A setback is just a setup for a comeback, quoted by Dr. Willie Jolley. I sought constructive feedback from trusted mentors and peers, using it to refine my skills and strengthen my resolve. Over time, I developed a thicker skin and a more resilient mindset, essential traits for anyone pursuing a career in public speaking. I realized that my self-doubt came from fear of failure, fear of rejection, and feeling I wasn't perfect or not good enough. So, I had to adjust my mindset. Here are three simple things that I did to change my mindset:

Step 1: Get out of the comfort zone; do something that I wasn't comfortable doing

Step 2: Get into the learning zone; invest in myself and build my speaking skills

Step 3: Get into the growth zone; connect with other like-minded individuals excelling in their speaking careers.

The Pivotal Moment: My First Public Speaking Engagement

My first speaking engagement was actually a FREE event. I learned very quickly that if people didn't know me or had not heard me speak before, they were not always willing to pay me to speak. So, I had to do a lot of free speaking events. In this business, you will quickly learn that you must do a lot of free events to get to the FEE events.

The first significant milestone in my speaking career came when I was invited to be the soloist at a friend's wedding at the Duke University Chapel in Durham, NC. I was in my 30s then, and the invitation was thrilling and daunting. This was my first opportunity to sing to a large audience outside my familiar church environment. Although singing wasn't a speaking event, it was very similar, especially since I would be singing from the top of the Chapel, which is 210 feet tall with a 50-bell carillon and three pipe organs. Yes, the familiar feeling of butterflies in my stomach and my knees wobbling came back like I was seven years old again. As I approached the microphone to begin singing, I remembered that this was my time to shine, and I quickly forgot about the fear of making a mistake or the lack of confidence.

My first paid speaking event came unexpectedly when I was invited to a healthcare conference. I had applied to various conferences and events to speak with no success, so I was shocked when this speaking opportunity was approved. This opportunity allowed me to speak in front of an audience of 300 people for three days. By this time, the fear of failure was non-existent; however, the fear of rejection started to creep in. Speaking to individuals that I didn't know or had no connection with was a little daunting. During this time, I relied heavily on my 3 Steps of getting out of my comfort zone, into my learning zone, and focusing on my growth zone. This experience allowed me to share my knowledge with a new group of individuals, connect and network with others, and expand my speaking skills.

Preparation and Practice

Preparation for the wedding and the conference was intense. I spent weeks researching, writing, and rehearsing my songs and messages for the conference. I wanted to ensure my message was clear, impactful, and inspiring. I practiced in front of mirrors, rehearsed and recorded myself to analyze my delivery, and sought feedback from friends and mentors. This rigorous preparation was not just about perfecting my singing or delivering an impactful message but also about building the confidence to stand in front of a large audience and deliver my message with conviction.

The Experience of Speaking

The conference day arrived, and I was a bundle of nerves. As I stood backstage, waiting for my turn to speak, I could hear the murmur of the audience and feel the energy in the room. When my name was called, I took a deep breath and walked onto the stage. The bright lights and the sea of faces were intimidating, but something shifted as I began to speak. I felt a connection with the audience and a sense of shared purpose and understanding. My nerves melted away, and I delivered my speech with passion and clarity. The applause and positive feedback that followed were overwhelming. A positive experience on day one made speaking easier for the next two days. This experience was a turning point for me, solidifying my desire to pursue a career in public speaking.

Lessons Learned and Key Takeaways

Several key lessons stand out after my journey from a shy country girl singing in church to a confident international public speaker. These lessons apply to speaking and any endeavor that requires stepping out of one's comfort zone and embracing new challenges.

Lesson #1: The Importance of Support Systems

Having a strong support system is crucial. My family, church community and mentors played a significant role in encouraging and guiding me. They provided a safe space for me to grow and learn, offering constructive feedback and celebrating my successes. Surrounding yourself with supportive, like-minded, and positive people can make a significant difference in your journey.

Lesson #2: Embracing Failure as a Learning Opportunity

Failure is an inevitable part of any journey. I made mistakes, faced criticism, and experienced setbacks, but each failure taught me valuable lessons and helped me improve. Embracing failure as a learning opportunity rather than a defeat is essential for growth and development. Remember that failure is the first step towards success.

Lesson #3: Authenticity and Energy

Authenticity and energy are the cornerstones of effective speaking. People connect with genuine and energetic speakers who are true to themselves. Finding your unique voice and speaking from the heart can make your message more impactful and memorable. Remember, share stories about your experience with your audience so they can build a connection with you. Don't be boring!

Lesson #4: The Power of Preparation

Preparation is the key to success. Whether singing in church or speaking at a conference, thorough preparation gave me the confidence and competence to perform well. Investing time, money, and effort in preparation can significantly enhance your performance and outcomes. Sometimes, you must invest in yourself financially to get where you want to be. Having a speaking coach/mentor and/or participating in a speaking mastermind can benefit your speaking career.

Conclusion

Starting a speaking career involves challenges, growth, and self-discovery. My journey began with singing in church at the age of seven, a humble start that taught me invaluable lessons about confidence, authenticity, and resilience. Each experience, from overcoming stage fright to delivering my first public speech, has shaped me into the speaker I am today. As I continue on this path, I carry with me the lessons learned and the unwavering belief that if you BET on yourself, anything is possible. Believe in yourself, Get Excited about speaking, and Take action on speaking opportunities that come your way.

Your next Steps!

Let's begin with four simple steps:

Step #1- Know what you want

Know what your "why" is. Ensure you clarify and understand how your personal goals align with your speaking goals. Ask yourself, what is most important?

Step #2 – Create a plan

Determine what skills you need, determine your speaking goals, and then develop a plan to achieve them.

Step#3 – Be Accountable

Clarify the actions that will grow your speaking business and move you forward. Build your networks and track your progress.

Step#4 – Take Action

Let's get started! Always remember to track your progress!

Another important step is to write out your vision statement and ensure that it aligns with your speaking business goals.

If you can dream it, you can achieve it

DR. LINDA R. JORDON

Dr. Linda R Jordon is a highly sought-after international speaker, leadership expert, coach, trainer, and author. With over 30 years of professional leadership, Dr. Jordon created LRJ Coaching & Business Solutions, LLC, to help women change their mindset, improve their communication skills, and live their best lives. Dr. Jordon inspires clients to illuminate their potential by turning challenges into opportunities to have the lives they deserve. She helps clients transition from corporate life to being their own boss. You can connect with Dr. Jordon through the following channels:

Email: linda@lrj-consulting.com
Website: www.lindajordon.com
Instagram: @drlindarjordon
Facebook: Linda.Jordon2

Chapter Seven

REDEFINING SUCCESS FOR RETURNING CITIZENS: FROM INCARCERATION TO INSPIRATION

REV. DR. ROGER E. DIXON SR.

What if I were to ask you the question, "What does success mean to you?" Many of you would respond that a certain amount of money, a certain level of education, reaching a certain status, or acquiring specific material possessions are important goals. Rev. Dr. Roger E. Dixon, Sr., success isn't determined by external measures such as money, power, or status. Nor is it defined by the adversities of your past experiences or current circumstances. Instead, it is determined by the ability to work in your unique lane of genius and make a positive impact in the lives of others. Success to him is living with authenticity and sharing your gifts so that you leave a legacy that will inspire future generations for years to come.

Rev. Dixon's work in the prison ministry is a testament to his profound understanding of true success. For over 30 years, he has dedicated his life to guiding incarcerated individuals and returning citizens toward a path of genuine success. Through his unwavering commitment and compassionate mentorship, he has transformed countless lives, helping them to overcome the stigma of their past and embrace a future filled with potential and purpose.

In this chapter, we delve into Rev. Dixon's remarkable journey as he empowers incarcerated people to achieve success and lead productive lives as contributing members of their communities. His innovative approach goes beyond mere rehabilitation; it is about instilling a deep sense of self-worth, fostering resilience, and equipping individuals with the tools they need to thrive. By encouraging them to discover and cultivate their unique talents, Rev. Dixon ensures their contributions to society are meaningful and impactful.

Rev. Dixon's philosophy centers on the belief that every person, regardless of their past, can succeed. His work with returning citizens underscores the importance of second chances and the transformative power of empathy and support. Through his four SUCCESS principles, he has built a legacy of hope and empowerment, showing that success is not confined by circumstances but is defined by one's ability to influence the world positively.

As we explore the stories of those whose lives have been changed by Rev. Dixon's ministry, we witness a powerful narrative of redemption and renewal. These individuals, once confined by the walls of their past, now stand as beacons of possibility, proving that anyone can achieve greatness with the proper guidance and determination. From James, who rose from a cook to a head chef, to Nicole, who found a job as a waitress and became a mother, their resilience is truly inspiring. Rev. Dixon's dedication to prison ministry changes lives and reshapes communities, creating a ripple effect that extends far beyond the prison walls.

This chapter celebrates Rev. Roger E. Dixon, Sr.'s extraordinary work and the enduring impact he has on the lives of returning citizens. It is a tribute to his belief in the inherent potential within every individual and his relentless pursuit of a world where success is defined by the positive legacy we leave behind. Through his ministry, Rev. Dixon teaches us that true success is found in the lives we touch and the hope we inspire in others.

The Transformational Success Story of James

Rev. Dixon vividly recalls the story of James, an inmate caught in a cycle of incarceration. Upon meeting James, Rev. Dixon invited him to join his Monday night Men's Prison Ministry Group. James found solace and inspiration in the group, so much so that he vowed to Rev.

Dixon that one day he would make a significant difference in his community upon release.

True to his word, when James was released, he secured a job as a cook at the local mission. Rev. Dixon didn't stop there; he continued visiting, mentoring, and supporting James, guiding him through his transformation journey. Under Rev. Dixon's mentorship, James became a role model, epitomizing the power of change and the essence of true success.

James's story is a powerful reminder that anyone can rise above their circumstances and make a lasting impact with the proper support and determination. It also underscores the importance of community support in the reintegration of returning citizens. Within a few short years, James advanced from cook to head chef at the mission, a testament to his dedication and growth. But his journey didn't end in the kitchen; James joined Rev. Dixon's ministry team, becoming a beacon of hope and a living example of redemption and triumph. His success is not just his own but a testament to the power of community support in the reentry process.

The Transformational Success Story of Nicole

Rev. Dixon's unwavering dedication and compassion shine through in the story of Nicole, a young woman referred to his Thursday night Women's Prison Ministry Group. At three months pregnant and without any prenatal care, Nicole reached out to Rev. Dixon in desperation. Moved by her plight, Rev. Dixon took immediate action, and by the next day, he had secured the necessary prenatal care for her.

Their connection didn't end there. After Nicole's release, Rev. Dixon continued to assist her by helping to secure baby clothing and formula. On Christmas Day, Nicole joyfully called Rev. Dixon to announce the birth of her beautiful baby girl, Brooke. True to his commitment, Rev. Dixon visited mother and daughter the next day, offering continued support and encouragement.

Nicole's story is a testament to the transformative power of Rev. Dixon's ministry. With his guidance, she secured a job as a restaurant waitress and is now leading a successful life, providing for her daughter and embodying the true meaning of resilience and hope. Nicole's journey under the compassionate mentorship of Rev. Dixon exemplifies the profound impact of second chances and unwavering support.

Your Future with Success Academy: Transforming Lives

Rev. Roger E. Dixon Sr. stands as a beacon of hope and transformation, dedicating over 30 years to uplifting previously incarcerated individuals. His journey as an award-winning keynote speaker, author, mentor, and entrepreneur has been marked by a steadfast commitment to helping others overcome obstacles and achieve their potential. Through his four SUCCESS principles, Rev. Dixon has not only guided countless men and women to build sustainable lives, attain gainful employment, pursue higher education, and emerge as leaders in their communities but also significantly impacted their communities. His work is a testament to the transformative power of individual and community empowerment, inspiring hope and optimism for the potential for positive change.

As a success coach and mentor to men ages 20-40 returning from the Criminal Justice System, Rev. Dixon established the "Your Future with Success Academy," which provides an opportunity for change through leadership training, education resources, employer referrals, family advocacy, and prison reform. This initiative is made possible through the collaborative efforts of community leaders, faith-based organizations, and intensive group coaching. Their collective support and commitment play a crucial role in helping returning citizens achieve success with these four factors: goals, optimism, focus, and perseverance to become your own success champion!

A Legacy of Compassion and Change

Rev. Dixon's work is deeply rooted in his passion for criminal justice reform and belief in redemption's power. As a leading voice in this movement, he has tirelessly advocated for the reintegration of formerly incarcerated individuals into society. His holistic approach addresses the practical aspects of reentry—such as employment and education—and the emotional and psychological challenges that many face upon release, instilling a sense of reassurance and confidence in their journey.

The foundation of Rev. Dixon's philosophy is his four SUCCESS principles: Spiritual grounding, Understanding one's potential, Commitment to personal growth, Continuous education, and Service to the community. These principles are theoretical concepts and practical tools implemented with remarkable success in his various programs and initiatives. This emphasis on practicality and effectiveness instills confidence in the potential for personal and community empowerment through these principles.

Spiritual Grounding: The First Step to Transformation

At the core of Rev. Dixon's approach is the belief that spiritual grounding provides a foundation for all other aspects of personal development. He emphasizes the importance of faith and spirituality in overcoming the trauma and hardships associated with incarceration. Through his Prison Ministry, Rev. Dixon offers spiritual guidance and support to incarcerated individuals, helping them reconnect with their inner selves and find a purpose.

This spiritual grounding is crucial in fostering resilience and hope. It helps individuals to see beyond their current circumstances and to believe in the possibility of a better future. Rev. Dixon's sermons and one-on-one counseling sessions are filled with messages of hope, forgiveness, and redemption, inspiring those he works with to envision and work toward a brighter future.

Understanding One's Potential: Unlocking Hidden Talents

Rev. Dixon's second principle, Understanding One's Potential, focuses on helping individuals recognize their inherent talents and abilities. Many who have been incarcerated struggle with low self-esteem and a lack of self-worth. Rev. Dixon works to change this narrative by highlighting each person's unique skills and strengths.

Rev. Dixon encourages individuals to explore their interests and talents through workshops and personal development programs. He provides opportunities for skill-building and personal growth, from vocational training to creative arts. By unlocking their potential, individuals are empowered to pursue new career paths and personal goals, transforming their lives meaningfully.

Commitment to Personal Growth: A Lifelong Journey

The third SUCCESS principle, Commitment to personal growth, emphasizes the importance of continuous self-improvement. Rev. Dixon instills in those he mentors a dedication to lifelong learning and development. This commitment is reflected in his various educational programs, which include GED preparation, college courses, and vocational training.

Rev. Dixon understands that personal growth is a journey that requires perseverance and dedication. He provides ongoing support and mentorship, helping individuals navigate their challenges. His emphasis on personal growth extends beyond the individual, fostering a culture of continuous improvement within families and communities.

Continuous Education: Empowering Through Knowledge

Continuous education is the fourth pillar of Rev. Dixon's SUCCESS principles. He believes that education is a powerful tool for empowerment and social change. Through his non-profit organization,

Heritage Community Outreach, Rev. Dixon has developed various educational programs for incarcerated individuals and at-risk youth.

These programs are designed to provide practical knowledge and skills directly applicable to real-world situations. Whether learning a trade, developing financial literacy, or gaining insights into personal health and wellness, Rev. Dixon's educational initiatives equip individuals with the tools they need to succeed.

Service to the Community: Giving Back and Leading by Example

The final principle, Service to the community, underscores the importance of giving back. Rev. Dixon believes that true success is about personal achievement and contributing to the greater good. He encourages those he mentors to become active members of their communities, using their experiences and skills to make a positive impact.

Rev. Dixon leads by example, dedicating much of his time to community service. His commitment to service is unwavering, whether through his work as a hospital chaplain, involvement in local schools as a substitute teacher, or leadership in various community organizations. He inspires others to follow in his footsteps, creating a ripple effect of positive change.

Heritage Community Outreach: A Lifeline for At-Risk Youth and Families

Heritage Community Outreach, the non-profit organization founded by Rev. Dixon, plays a pivotal role in its mission to support at-risk youth and families. The organization offers a range of programs designed to address the unique challenges faced by these groups. From mentorship and counseling services to educational and vocational training, Heritage Community Outreach provides a comprehensive support system for those in need.

One of the organization's flagship programs is its youth mentorship initiative, which pairs at-risk youth with positive role models. These mentors provide guidance, support, and encouragement, helping young people navigate the challenges of adolescence and build a foundation for future success. The program has effectively reduced dropout rates and increased college enrollment among participants.

Slam Dunk Your Future to Success: A Guide to Empowerment

Rev. Dixon's impact extends beyond his direct work with individuals and communities. He is also the author of "Slam Dunk Your Future to Success," a book that distills his SUCCESS principles into a practical guide for youth and young adults. The book offers insights and strategies for overcoming obstacles, setting and achieving goals, and building a successful and fulfilling life.

"Slam Dunk Your Future to Success" has been widely acclaimed for its accessible and actionable advice. It serves as a valuable resource for young people seeking direction and inspiration, as well as educators and mentors looking to support their students and mentees.

Prison Family Ministry: A Platform for Advocacy and Support

In addition to his work on the ground, Rev. Dixon created a platform for advocacy and support through his weekly podcast, "Prison Family Ministry." Broadcast live on www.thevoice17104.com and Facebook, the podcast addresses mass incarceration, unjust policies, and the challenges formerly incarcerated individuals and their families face.

The podcast features interviews with experts, activists, and individuals who have successfully navigated the reentry process. It provides a space for open and honest dialogue about the realities of incarceration and reentry, advocating for policy changes and offering practical advice and support for listeners. Through "Prison Family Ministry," Rev. Dixon continues to raise awareness about mass incarceration's impact and promote a more just and compassionate society.

Recognizing Rev. Dixon's Contributions

Rev. Dixon's work has not gone unnoticed. He has received numerous awards and accolades for his leadership and contributions to his community. His efforts have been featured in leading newspapers and magazines, including New York Weekly, CEO Weekly, and Harrisburg Magazine. These recognitions highlight the significant impact of Rev. Dixon on individuals and communities.

His inspirational speeches have captivated audiences on both live and virtual international stages, including prominent events such as Shawn Fair's Leadership Experience Tour, Trevor Otts's Black CEO Summit, Ryan Greene's Make It Matter, and the Harrisburg Community Conference. Through these platforms, Rev. Dixon has shared his message of hope, redemption, and empowerment with a global audience.

Conclusion: The Legacy of Rev. Dr. Roger E. Dixon Sr.

Rev. Roger E. Dixon Sr. embodies the spirit of resilience, compassion, and unwavering dedication to helping others. Through his Prison Ministry, Heritage Community Outreach, and various educational and advocacy initiatives, he has transformed countless lives and inspired a movement towards redemption and empowerment.

His work with previously incarcerated individuals is a testament to the power of second chances and the potential for personal transformation. By providing spiritual grounding, fostering personal growth, promoting continuous education, and encouraging service to the community, Rev. Dixon has created a blueprint for success that transcends the confines of incarceration and extends into every aspect of life.

Key Takeaways

1. Spiritual Grounding: A solid spiritual foundation is crucial for personal transformation and resilience.
2. Recognizing Potential: Helping individuals understand and unlock their unique talents and abilities can lead to meaningful personal and professional growth.
3. Commitment to Growth: Continuous personal development and lifelong learning are essential for success.
4. Education as Empowerment: Providing practical knowledge and skills through education empowers individuals to build successful and fulfilling lives.
5. Community Service: True success involves giving back to the community and making a positive impact on the lives of others.

REV. DR. ROGER E. DIXON SR.

Rev Dr. Roger E. Dixon Sr. is the Moderator and preacher at Harrisburg First Church of the Brethren in Harrisburg, Pennsylvania, and the founder of Your Future Success Academy. The Academy helps returning citizens find success after prison. He is an inspirational figure, entrepreneur, substitute teacher, community leader, prison mentor, hospital chaplain, and advocate.

Throughout his career, he has made significant strides across industries, from teaching business strategies to aspirants to funding youth projects and other philanthropic pursuits.

Dr. Dixon's extensive 30 years of experience have made a profound impact on various communities, particularly those released from prison and striving for a better life. His founding of a non-profit organization, Heritage Community Outreach, stands as a testament to his unwavering commitment to helping others thrive.

You can find Dr. Dixon on Facebook, Instagram, X, and LinkedIn—all under Rev Dr. Roger E. Dixon Sr.

Website: https://revrogerdixonsr.com/
Email: rdixon532000@yahoo.com
Facebook: https://www.facebook.com/roger.dixon5
LinkedIn: linkedin.com/in/dr-roger-e-dixon-sr-a6825142

Chapter Eight

FROM SHADOWS TO SHINE

PAULA BURCH JACKSON

Have you ever wondered why you do some of the things you do? Why do you think the way you think? Or why certain things trigger emotions within you that cause you to respond in a way that is out of character? Well, I certainly have. One day, while strolling through REELs on Facebook, I discovered my answer when a video of a toddler seeing her shadow for the first time caught my attention. The sight of her shadow terrified her, and she began to frantically run away from it, only to realize that no matter how fast she ran, she could not outrun herself—this simple yet profound moment sparked a revelation. The little girl being afraid of her shadow became a metaphor that revealed, just as the toddler in the video was startled and frightened by her own shadow, we too can sometimes be afraid or uncomfortable with the dark side of ourselves that we may not fully understand, try to keep hidden or attempt to run away from.

Our dark side or shadow self refers to those aspects of our personality, thoughts, and emotions that we may find difficult to accept or acknowledge. These can include our fears, insecurities, negative emotions, desires, or behaviors that society has deemed unacceptable or undesirable. Just like the toddler running away from her shadow, we try to avoid or suppress these aspects of ourselves, thinking that by doing so, we can distance ourselves from them. However, much like the toddler's realization that she cannot outrun her shadow, we eventually understand that we cannot escape or ignore our dark side forever.

Eventually, a ray of light will shine on those dark areas, and we must be able to respond to the shadow without losing our authenticity. Our shadows are a part of us, and acknowledging and accepting them is an essential step toward self-awareness, growth, and personal development. By facing shadows of fears, insecurities, and negative emotions, we can begin to understand them, learn from them, and integrate them into our overall sense of self.

Carl Jung, a famous Swiss psychologist, described shadows as the parts of our personality that hold traits, emotions, and behaviors we try to ignore or hide because we have been conditioned to believe they are undesirable. These shadows represent the hidden aspects of ourselves that we tend to avoid acknowledging, leading us to avoid facing our inner fears, insecurities, or darker sides. Despite our efforts to distance ourselves from these shadows, they remain a fundamental part of who we are. When we neglect or deny our shadows, it can negatively impact our actions and emotions, causing us to react strongly to specific situations or behave in ways that are out of character. Recognizing and accepting our shadow is crucial for personal growth and self-awareness, allowing us to understand ourselves better.

As my awareness and understanding of shadows grew, I became adept at recognizing when a shadow was emerging. Yet, I was still trying to figure out how these shadows developed and how to transform them into strengths. Anger stood out the most among the shadows that pushed me out of character. I could vividly recall numerous occasions when I overreacted to seemingly trivial situations, my response disproportionate to the circumstances. In my quest to unravel the origins of my anger, I gleaned valuable insights from my 2-year-old granddaughter, Annalee.

One day, Annalee was upset when her father refused to give her a snack. It was the first time I had witnessed her in what my mother would have called a temper tantrum. She threw herself on the floor, wailing and screaming at the top of her lungs. Concerned for her well-being, I was suddenly reminded of how my mother had handled my tantrums. I recalled how my mother would reach for a belt, a shoe, or any nearby object, threatening to give me a reason to be upset. These experiences had taught me to suppress my anger. Although I had unwittingly repeated this pattern with my children, I was pleasantly surprised to observe my son taking a different approach with Annalee.

After witnessing my son's calm and empathetic response to Annalee's tantrum, I was struck by the realization that my struggles with anger were deeply rooted in my upbringing. Instead of resorting to threats, my son knelt to Annalee's level and gently reassured her, "Annalee, patience. You can have it, just not right now." Surprisingly, Annalee responded with understanding, saying, "Okay, Daddy," and followed his guidance to take deep breaths. Within moments, she composed herself and resumed playing as if nothing had occurred. This display of emotional management in a two-year-old child highlighted the authenticity and innocence that define this stage of development, often wrongly labeled as "the terrible twos" by society, which tends to suppress natural expressions of emotion.

A few weeks later, when Annalee stayed overnight with me, she encountered some challenges during her potty-training phase, leading to several accidents despite my reminders. Frustrated after the second accident, I raised my voice and questioned her actions. In a surprising turn of events, Annalee calmly responded, "Sweet P, are you angry?" Taken aback, I acknowledged my frustration, and she gently suggested, "Okay, let's breathe." Guided by her, we engaged in three rounds of deep breathing. Following this calming exercise, she inquired, "Sweet P, are you better now?" This poignant interaction revealed the profound impact of my son's teachings on emotional regulation. It underscored how Annalee had internalized these lessons to manage her emotions and recognize and assist others in navigating their emotional challenges.

Through my experiences with Annalee, I understood that breaking the cycle of negative shadows starts with acknowledgment, understanding, and compassion. This process of transformation fundamentally alters how we react not only to ourselves but also to others. Recognizing and accepting our shadows pave the way for emotional growth and healthier interactions with those around us. Embracing empathy and compassion as we navigate our inner struggles fosters personal development and cultivates deeper connections and understanding in our relationships with others. Annalee's emotional awareness and management lessons were a powerful reminder that we can foster a more positive and harmonious way of engaging with ourselves and the world by approaching our shadows with kindness and insight. This journey of self-discovery and empathy offers us the opportunity to break free from the constraints of our shadows and embrace a path of personal growth and authentic connection through shadow work.

Engaging in shadow work has guided me on a path of self-discovery, healing, and personal growth like never before. By delving into the depths of my psyche to confront and integrate my shadows, I have gained a deeper understanding of myself, my motivations, and my behaviors. This process has allowed me to release long-held emotional baggage, overcome self-limiting beliefs, and cultivate a greater inner peace and authenticity. Through shadow work, I have learned to embrace all facets of my being, including the parts I once considered undesirable or uncomfortable.

This acceptance has empowered me to navigate life's challenges with resilience and compassion, fostering a more profound connection with myself and others. Shadow work is essential because it enables us to confront our inner darkness, heal past wounds, and cultivate a more balanced and integrated sense of self. By shining a light on our shadows and embracing them with love and understanding, we can transcend limitations, foster personal growth, and embark on a profound self-discovery and transformation journey.

Shadow work is an essential process for personal growth. It involves self-awareness, introspection, identifying and acknowledging shadow aspects, integrating them, and cultivating self-compassion and acceptance. In my coaching practice, I guide clients through a structured two-part process to support their journey toward self-discovery and transformation.

Part One: Chasing, Facing, and Embracing Your Shadows

1. **Chasing:** Chasing in shadow work means actively tracing back the roots of your shadows to uncover their origins. It involves delving into past experiences, memories, or situations where you first began to repress emotions or aspects of yourself that contributed to forming these shadows. This process involves helping clients identify the initial seeds of these shadows to determine whether they stem from childhood experiences, societal conditioning, trauma, or other significant life events.

2. **Facing:** Once identified, facing your shadows requires courage and honesty. It involves confronting these aspects of yourself without judgment, blame, or evasion. This step often includes acknowledging uncomfortable truths, past traumas, fears, or negative beliefs contributing to your shadow self. Facing your shadows is crucial for gaining deeper self-awareness and understanding. Clients are guided to confront these shadow aspects without judgment, which involves exploring past experiences and emotions to understand how these hidden parts have influenced their behaviors and decisions.

3. **Embracing:** Embracing your shadows means accepting them as integral parts of your identity. It's about integrating these aspects into your self-concept rather than denying or suppressing them. This step fosters self-compassion and empathy towards yourself, recognizing that shadows carry valuable lessons and potential for growth. Embracing shadows allows for greater authenticity and inner harmony. Clients learn to accept these aspects as part of their whole self, fostering a sense of completeness and self-compassion. This acceptance is facilitated through compassionate dialogue and therapeutic techniques.

Part Two: Taking ACTION framework

1. **A - Acknowledge & Acceptance:** Begin by recognizing and accepting your shadows without judgment or resistance. This step involves acknowledging their presence in your life and the emotions they evoke. By accepting your shadows, you create space for self-awareness and growth.

2. **C - Compassion:** Approach yourself with kindness and gentleness throughout the shadow work process. Offer self-compassion and understanding as you navigate through challenging emotions and experiences associated with your shadows. Compassion fosters healing and allows you to embrace your vulnerabilities with greater resilience.

3. **T - Transformation:** Embrace the potential for transformation that comes with integrating your shadows. View your shadows not as flaws but as opportunities for growth, learning, and positive change. Transformation occurs as you incorporate the lessons and insights from your shadows into your personal development journey.

4. **I - Insight & Inquiry:** This means seeking insights into your shadows' root causes and underlying patterns. Engage in self-inquiry by asking probing questions to deepen your understanding. Explore the beliefs, experiences, or traumas that have contributed to forming your shadows. Insight and inquiry facilitate self-discovery and help uncover hidden aspects of your psyche.

5. **O - Openness & Observation:** Cultivate openness to fully explore your shadows without judgment or fear. Observe your thoughts, feelings, and behaviors associated with your shadows with curiosity and awareness. Being open allows you to embrace vulnerability and authenticity, creating space for deeper self-exploration and healing.

6. **N—Nurture & Navigating:** Nurture yourself throughout the process of shadow integration by practicing self-care and prioritizing activities that nourish your physical, emotional, and spiritual well-being. Seek support from trusted individuals such as friends, family, or therapists who can provide guidance

and encouragement. Navigating challenges with patience and resilience lets you stay committed to your growth journey.

Taking ACTION in shadow work will foster personal transformation and emotional healing, allowing you to pave the way for profound self-discovery and empowerment. From gaining insights to nurturing yourself, each step is vital in your journey toward greater self-awareness, authenticity, and inner peace.

How to Work with Me

If you're ready to embark on this transformative journey of shadow work, I invite you to connect with me. We can explore and integrate your shadow aspects through personalized coaching sessions, workshops, or group programs, leading to a more authentic and fulfilling life.

To work with me, you can:

- **Book a Session:** Visit my website to schedule a one-on-one coaching session tailored to your unique needs.
- **Join a Workshop:** Participate in interactive workshops to delve deeply into shadow work principles.
- **Engage in Group Sessions:** Join a supportive community where we explore shadow work together in a group setting.
- Embrace your shadow, transform your life, and discover the power within you. Let's begin this journey together. Contact me through my website or directly to start your path toward self-discovery and personal growth.

HOW I WORK:

Organizations: I collaborate with organizations committed to cultivating exceptional leadership. Through shadow work, leaders can gain profound self-awareness, understand their strengths and weaknesses, and develop authentic leadership styles. By embracing their shadows, leaders foster a culture of empathy, resilience, and innovation within their teams.

Couples: Shadow work provides a transformative journey for couples seeking more profound connection and understanding. By exploring individual shadows together, I help couples enhance communication, resolve conflicts more effectively, and cultivate a relationship grounded in empathy and mutual growth.

Faith-Based Organizations: I partner with faith-based organizations to integrate shadow work into spiritual growth and community development. By addressing hidden fears, doubts, and judgments, individuals can deepen their spiritual connection, embody compassion, and live authentically aligned with their faith principles.

Individuals: If you're on a journey to self-discovery and healing, shadow work offers profound benefits. It enables you to work in small groups or one-on-one to uncover unconscious patterns, heal past wounds, and reclaim lost aspects of yourself. You can cultivate inner peace, resilience, and a renewed sense of purpose through shadow integration.

PAULA BURCH JACKSON, MA

Paula Burch Jackson (Coach PBJ) is an empowerment strategist, transformational life coach, author, and ordained minister dedicated to guiding individuals and organizations through the transformative process of shadow work. With a passion for empowering others to embrace their shadows as pathways to personal growth and authenticity, Paula specializes in cultivating self-awareness, emotional healing, and leadership development. Through her coaching programs and workshops, Paula helps clients uncover hidden potentials, heal past wounds, and navigate life transitions with resilience and clarity. Paula's holistic approach integrates spiritual wisdom, insights, and practical strategies to support individuals toward a more fulfilling and purpose-driven life. Whether working with leaders, couples, or individuals seeking personal transformation, Paula fosters empathy, empowerment, and spiritual alignment.

Website: www.coachpbj.com
Email: info@coachpbjspeaks.com
LinkedIn: linkedin.com/in/coachpbj
Instagram: https://www.instagram.com/coach_pbj/
Facebook: https://www.facebook.com/paula.
            burch?mibextid=LQQJ4d

Chapter Nine

FROM THE BLOCK TO THE BOARDROOM: UNLEASHING LEADERSHIP POWER AS A 6'5 AFRO-LATINO FROM EASTSIDE DETROIT

JERMAINE STANLEY

Introduction

This chapter bridges two disparate worlds—the gritty streets of Eastside Detroit and the polished corridors of corporate America—revealing how adversity fosters resilient leadership. It traces my journey as a young Afro-Latino, leveraging a unique background and formidable challenges into a leadership path marked by resilience, adaptability, and integrity.

In each section, you'll discover the impact of socio-economic and racial dynamics on leadership through my experiences with code-switching, striving for authenticity in conformist environments, and the profound role of cultural identity in professional growth.

From overcoming poverty and discrimination to mastering corporate politics, this narrative not only shares my personal triumphs and trials but also reflects broader truths about navigating and transforming the landscapes of leadership—whether you are leading a small team, a large corporation, or yourself.

Forged in Adversity: A Journey of Resilience and Leadership

Growing up as an Afro-Latino in Eastside Detroit and navigating the complexities of code-switching and corporate America provided me with invaluable lessons that have shaped my leadership journey. These early experiences taught me perseverance, resilience, and the importance of self-reliance—qualities that are essential for any leader.

During my college years at Alabama A&M University (A&M), I took on summer jobs to support myself and gain experience. One of the most memorable was working as a field sales rep for Columbus Energy Concepts in Columbus, Ohio. I did that for two summers.

That first summer, I worked tirelessly, saved every penny possible, and stayed with my aunt and cousins—making sure to contribute as much as possible to that household. My main goal then was to buy my first car, and I did—a used, white 1987 Chevy Z24 with tinted windows and a manual transmission that the saleswoman who sold it to me taught me how to drive the day I bought the car!

I was thrilled to return to the same job the following summer, but my circumstances had changed. I could no longer stay at my aunt's house. Desperate for a place to rest after driving all night from Michigan, I ended up at a crack house where I knew some people who would let me rest my head for free. Now, these weren't strangers, so I trusted them, but that lifestyle is just not who I am. Never has been. Still, I was very grateful for their hospitality.

And let me tell you. At that crack house, I saw it all. To minimize my time there, I would stay out all day—as long as I could, mostly living out of my car and showering at Ohio State University's Larkins rec center. At the rec center, I stayed healthy and out of trouble by working out and playing basketball daily. Doing so helped me keep my mind right despite the chaos.

At times, the situation at the crack house became too volatile, forcing me to find cheap motels for a safer night's rest. Eventually,

I found shared housing with a few other students, where I felt safer and more comfortable. But one night, before I made it out of that already dangerous situation, I came up against a harrowing ordeal with the police.

Those same friends from the crack house had rented a few rooms at a motel in Reynoldsburg, Ohio, to hang out and watch the Bulls versus the Phoenix Suns. After the game, as I was driving back "home," in the middle of the night on I-270, I saw a rush of police lights on the opposite side of the road. Before I knew it, those same lights had crossed the median and now headed towards me.

They pulled me over, had the drugs dogs out, and went through all my stuff. It turns out they had been surveilling my friends and me at the motel and thought I might be involved in some drug operation. They let me go eventually, but that whole thing was downright terrifying (cue the history of policing black bodies in the U.S.). Plus, at the time, with no cell phones, I couldn't reach out to anyone and continued driving "home" alone in complete, horrified silence.

The message I am trying to convey is PERSEVERANCE! Whether you're leading yourself or others, you must keep pushing forward even (and especially) when things don't go your way. Focus on your goals, not what stands in your way.

Those summers in Columbus taught me the importance of endurance and resilience—qualities that have been vital in my leadership journey. No matter the obstacles, a leader must always find a way to move forward and stay focused on their goals. As a young man trying to survive with what little he had while building a better future for himself, I didn't let anything derail me from my dreams and aspirations.

The Token Challenge: Navigating Identity and Inclusion in Corporate America

After finishing my undergraduate studies, I had always envisioned myself thriving in corporate America. Growing up in Detroit during the 80s, I was surrounded by the proliferation of drugs and crime.

Many of my friends were caught up in that world, but I always wanted something different for myself. My dream was to be the big boss in the corner office, with my feet on the desk, calling the shots. But when I finally got there, I was quickly humbled by the reality of my situation.

Starting on the sales floor at Ameritech, where I sold Yellow Pages advertising and websites, I was among the few people of color. I learned very quickly that I had to work two to three times as hard as my white counterparts just to be seen as (barely) equal. And even when I managed to carve out a place for myself, I was still often seen as the "token negro" rather than a truly integral part of the team. So, to fit in, I found myself code-switching often—changing how I looked, talked, and walked (a struggle that, for me, persisted until the early 2010s and for many others, persists today).

Despite having the same qualifications, tenure, and often a better track record than my peers, I was repeatedly passed over for promotions. The corporate line was always the same: "Maybe next year will be your year."

Sure. Maybe next year, I'll become a white man, I thought.

As a leader, I find myself pulled in multiple directions. On one side, people like me—brown and black— are urging me not to sell out. On the other side, some are not like me, trying to mold me into someone they are comfortable with, an "Uncle Tom" or "Obama," as they say. But pleasing everyone is an impossible task.

The journey is far from over, and much work remains to be done. However, the lessons from my early years continue to guide me in navigating these challenges and striving for equity and representation in leadership. I hope you can learn something from them, too.

Leadership at the Crossroads: Integrity, Inclusion, and the Art of Balance

Integrity and honesty are the cornerstones of effective leadership. They define who you are, how you are perceived, and how you will be remembered. Without them, others might be hesitant to work with you or support your vision, while embodying them inspires trust and motivation, essential for achieving your goals. Leadership without integrity and honesty is unsustainable, and staying true to these values requires deep reflection and steadfast commitment.

Integrity involves doing the right thing even when no one is watching, being transparent, owning mistakes, and learning from them. Honesty complements this by requiring open and truthful communication with your team, stakeholders, and yourself. Leading with integrity and honesty fosters a culture of trust and respect, which is vital for long-term success and a positive work environment.

Balancing the needs and expectations of your team is a significant leadership challenge. You must care for those who support you and ensure effective project execution, but always pleasing everyone is impossible. It's crucial to regularly self-reflect, remain faithful to your values, and make decisions that align with the best interests of your organization. Open communication and realistic management of expectations are key, as well as always acknowledging and accepting that not everyone will be satisfied, and that's OK.

Tough Choices: Integrity and Resolve in Leadership Decisions

Making sound decisions while adhering to your principles is crucial for maintaining trust and respect within your team.

As a leader, some of the decisions you'll face will be straightforward, such as approving a budget or scheduling a meeting. However, the true test of leadership comes with the more challenging decisions like restructuring a team, implementing a new strategy, or navigating a crisis. These decisions often involve considerable risk and can significantly impact the organization.

Then, there are the unpopular decisions. These are perhaps the *most* difficult, as they can lead to dissent and discomfort within the team. Examples include downsizing, cutting costs, or enforcing strict policies.

Despite their unpopularity, such decisions are sometimes necessary for the long-term health and success of an organization.

When making decisions, it is critical not to let others influence you in ways that compromise your core values. Maintaining trust and respect within your team depends on your ability to be consistent and principled in your decision-making process.

Pressure from stakeholders, peers, or even team members can be intense. It is easy to succumb to demands against your better judgment to please others. However, compromising your principles for short-term gains or to avoid conflict can erode trust and respect in the long run.

In making tough or unpopular decisions, it is crucial to communicate openly and transparently to gain understanding and, ultimately, acceptance from your team, even if they disagree with the decision.

From Potential to Performance: Leading Through Talent Development

A critical aspect of leadership is recognizing and nurturing talent within your team. This means identifying and promoting self-starters, managing underperformers, and leveraging each team member's strengths to build a more cohesive and effective unit.

Self-starters, or "doers," are vital as they drive projects forward independently and are often the backbone of a successful team. Recognizing these individuals involves noting who consistently delivers results, rises to challenges, and seeks improvement. Promoting these talents early maximizes their impact and encourages a culture of proactivity and accountability.

Conversely, managing underperformers is crucial, as their lack of productivity can also affect team morale. Effective management starts with honest, constructive feedback and support for improvement. Sometimes, repositioning a team member to a role better suited to their strengths can enhance both their performance and job satisfaction.

Like a skilled coach, a good leader must align team members with roles that match their skills. For instance, you wouldn't make someone who excels in dribbling and passing the main shooter on a basketball team.

Cultivating Harmony: Proactive Leadership Against Workplace Drama

My next piece of advice? Leave the drama for your momma! It has no place in any organization, and you must root it out *immediately* as a leader. Allowing drama to fester is like letting cancer or a virus proliferate within your team. If not addressed immediately, it can cause irreparable damage to your organizational culture and your legacy as a leader.

Drama creates unnecessary distractions, hampers productivity, and significantly damages team morale. If unchecked, drama can create a toxic environment where trust and respect are eroded. As a leader, you must be proactive and decisive in addressing any signs of drama as soon as they arise. If you don't, that drama can quickly become unmanageable and challenging to mend. It can also make you appear weak and ineffective as a leader.

To avoid this, make it known to your team that you strive to maintain a positive and harmonious environment for everyone, which requires that all interactions remain respectful and constructive. Also, ensure that any issues will be addressed promptly and fairly.

The Well-Balanced Leader: Prioritizing Health for Effective Leadership

Your mental, physical, and spiritual health are the foundations of your ability to lead (both professionally and as the CEO of your own life). And you are no good to anyone—whether it's yourself, your family, or the organizations you lead—if you are not at your best.

Feeling good physically helps me stay focused and disciplined. A healthy lifestyle, including regular exercise and a balanced diet, boosts my energy levels, enhances my mood, and improves my overall health, making it easier to tackle the daily challenges of leadership with greater stamina and better results.

Mental well-being is equally critical. Each morning, at the same time, I dedicate 10 to 15 minutes to meditating. This practice helps me clear my mind, reduce stress, and maintain the clarity needed to face any challenges that come my way.

Finally, your spiritual health is another vital component of overall well-being. Whether it's spending time in nature, practicing mindfulness, or engaging in activities that bring joy and fulfillment, nurturing your spirit is essential for maintaining balance in your life—both in and out of the office.

Mastering the Art of Feedback: Navigating Criticism in Leadership

As a leader, criticism is inevitable. The key is to navigate it in a way that fosters growth and improvement while maintaining your focus.

Though sometimes painful, constructive criticism is essential for personal and professional growth. It provides valuable insights that can help you improve your performance and leadership skills and usually comes with specific suggestions and actionable advice. Recognizing and acting on the value of these critiques can significantly enhance your effectiveness as a leader.

On the other hand, not all criticism is constructive. Some feedback could be more specific, biased, or delivered with the intent to undermine rather than improve. This type of criticism can be particularly frustrating. It's important to be vigilant and discerning about the feedback you receive. Not all criticism deserves your energy and attention.

When faced with criticism, ask yourself, is the feedback coming from someone with your best interests at heart or someone with a personal agenda? This will help you determine if and how to respond. If the criticism is valid and presents an opportunity for growth, address it constructively. Make the necessary changes and communicate your actions transparently to build trust and demonstrate accountability.

Adopt a more strategic approach to unhelpful criticism. Understand why it was given and whether there's any truth to it, even if it was poorly delivered. If there's nothing constructive to glean, it's best just to acknowledge it and move on.

5 Key Takeaways from My Leadership Journey

Leadership, both for self and for others, is a continuous journey filled with daily opportunities to learn about yourself, your team, and your organization. The lessons you gather along the way, good and bad, collectively contribute to your growth as a leader. One profound piece of advice I received from a colleague recently captures this essence perfectly: "Your skin will grow back." It's a reminder that setbacks and challenges are only temporary.

Here are the five key takeaways I want you to take away from my story.

1. Admit Your Mistakes
No leader is perfect, and everyone makes errors. Owning up to your mistakes shows integrity and accountability. Learning from these missteps is essential and taking corrective action where possible. This not only helps you grow but also builds trust within your team.

2. Do Not Scorch the Earth
In pursuing success, avoid actions that harm relationships or the organizational culture just to get ahead. Sustainable success is built on respect, collaboration, and ethical behavior. Burning bridges might offer a short-term advantage but can lead to long-term repercussions undermining your leadership.

3. Find Common Ground

While finding common ground is often beneficial, it's not always possible or even desirable. Leadership sometimes requires making tough, unpopular decisions that go against the norm. These decisions are often necessary for the greater good of the organization. Staying firm and making difficult choices, even in the face of opposition, is a hallmark of strong leadership.

4. Trust Your Instincts

Over the years, I've learned to listen to my gut feelings, and this is advice I pass on to my children. If something doesn't feel right, it's probably a good idea to move on from it. Intuition, honed by experience, is a valuable tool in decision-making. It helps you navigate complex situations where data might be limited, but your inner sense guides you toward the best course of action.

5. Build a Circle of Trust

Surround yourself with people you can rely on to have your back and deliver on their commitments. These trusted advisors and colleagues provide support, diverse perspectives, and honest feedback. They help you see blind spots and offer a sounding board for ideas and strategies. A strong support network is a vital resource for any leader, enhancing personal and organizational resilience.

© 2024 Stanley Consulting Group

JERMAINE STANLEY

Jermaine Stanley is a Cybersecurity and IT Risk Advisory leader with over 25 years of experience working with Financial, Insurance, Non-Profit, and Government organizations. Jermaine is a member of ISACA Global's ISACA Foundation Board and recently served as President of the ISACA Greater Washington DC Chapter (ISACA GWDC).

Jermaine Stanley is a technology and thought leader and a champion of diversity, equity, and inclusion. His strong reputation for team building, mentoring, and creating Equitable and Inclusive cultures is a testament to his commitment. With a master's degree in software engineering, a Bachelor of Science in Electrical Engineering, CISA and CDPSE certifications, and a certification in Overcoming Unconscious Bias, Mr. Stanley is well-equipped to lead initiatives promoting DEI within organizations.

Jermaine is the Founder of Stanley Consulting Group, whose mission is to "ensure that the business leaders and employees we serve have the tools and insights to help them build diverse, inclusive, and equitable workplace environments."

Website: stanleyconsults.com
Email: jstanley@stanleyconaults.com
Facebook: https://www.facebook.com/StanleyConsults?mibextid=LQQJ4d
Instagram: jermainestanleyspeaks
LinkedIn: https://www.linkedin.com/company/stanley-consulting-group/
X: StanleyConsults

Chapter Ten

RISING FROM REJECTION
DR. TANIA'S JOURNEY TO FLOURISHING
DR. TANIA WHITE

Introduction

I am Dr. Tania, and I have always been my own worst critic. From a young age, praise from teachers and accolades from peers couldn't quell the quiet voice in my mind, whispering that I wasn't good enough. That whisper grew louder as I navigated my teens, becoming a relentless inner dialogue that colored every accomplishment with shades of doubt. Yet, my story is not just about the struggle; it's about my journey to silence that voice, discovering my true worth along the way. This tale is about overcoming self-doubt and finding the courage to self-reflect, believe in oneself, and FLOURISH.

I grew up in what's known as the Wild 100's in Chicago. From a young age, I stood out—whether it was my stellar grades, artistic flair, or prowess for cheer. My achievements should have been a source of celebration, but often, they were met with neglect. My attempts to seek approval and acceptance from my family were repeatedly met with indifference, fueling a deep-seated insecurity.

My brilliance was undeniable in school, yet I constantly needed to please others. I felt my friends often took my kindness for granted, using my reliability without reciprocating genuine friendship. Despite the exhaustive effort to excel and fit in, I faced exclusion. My heart ached with every sidelong glance and whispered conversation I wasn't part of.

II. Early Life and Rejection

My first taste of rejection came during my childhood when my half-sister would come to visit. She would be bold and overtake every room she entered. She would tell my friends lies about me to get them to stop talking with me and then laugh as I responded in frustration with tears and screaming at times. Even though my friends realized the lie and returned to speaking to me, the rejection hit me hard. It wasn't just about momentarily missing out on engaging with the kids in the neighborhood; it felt like confirmation of my deepest fears that I wasn't good enough. This initial rejection planted a seed of doubt that grew with each subsequent disappointment, fostering an ever-present fear of rejection and failure.

III. The People Pleasing Phase

I joined the church at a young age and learned I was blessed to be a blessing to others. I took this to heart, and by high school, I had perfected the art of people-pleasing. I was the model student, go-to for group projects, and trusted confidant for secrets. However, internally, I battled intense self-doubt. Every accolade came with a gnawing fear that I wasn't genuinely deserving, that without my relentless efforts to appease, I'd lose everything.

I had always aspired to be a blessing to others. Inspired by my compassionate grandmother, I yearned to make everyone around me happy and feel loved. In my eyes, being selfless and giving was the highest form of virtue. My kindness was genuine, but over time, it morphed into a compulsion for people-pleasing.

I joined the choir and numerous clubs in college and volunteered for countless events. I thrived on the appreciation and gratitude I received, which fueled my drive to do more. However, beneath the surface, I was struggling. The pressure to be a constant source of support for everyone weighed heavily on my shoulders. I often ignored my own needs, convinced it was a small price to pay for being a blessing to others.

IV. The Breaking Point

I, Dr. Tania, have always been the epitome of professionalism and grace. As the Chief Human Resources Officer at a major corporation, I was well-respected and known for my fairness and ability to manage complex situations. My team looked up to me, and my family adored me. However, beneath the polished exterior, I was struggling.

The company had recently undergone significant restructuring, the hiring of a new CEO, and the pressure on me had been mounting. My workload doubled, but my resources remained the same. On top of this, another new senior executive (a friend of the CEO) had joined the company. From the onset, this exec and the CEO made my life difficult, undermining my decisions, belittling me in meetings, and sending me emails laced with passive-aggressive remarks.

Determined to maintain my professionalism, I tried to take it in stride. I hoped I could earn their respect by performing my duties impeccably, but each day brought another round of harassment and dismissiveness.

Gradually, the stress started seeping into my personal life. I snapped at my loving husband and missed important events in my family's lives. I was there in person but emotionally absent, my mind perpetually tangled in work-related anxieties.

One holiday, after yet another grueling interaction with the executives, I returned to the brunch in frustration and responded to my family in an annoying and stressful manner. When I looked at my family's faces and body language, specifically my daughter's, I felt a wave of dread. My curt responses and angry demeanor shifted the mood away from a fun holiday brunch.

This realization hit me like a ton of bricks. I realized that my relentless efforts to keep everything together at work were causing my family to fall apart. I couldn't sleep that night, my mind racing with thoughts of my failures and the harassment I could no longer tolerate. Simultaneously, my personal life crumbled. My relationship, already strained from lack of time and emotional disconnection, reached a breaking point. Health issues emerged, igniting a crisis. One day, I broke down. I realized I had become a shadow of my true self, constantly bending to avoid conflict and rejection.

The next few days marked my breaking point. During a meeting, the exec publicly undermined me yet again, dismissing my expertise and recommendations. The stress and humiliation boiled over to the weekend. I sat at my dining room table that Sunday evening and vowed that I deserved respect and dignity and would no longer tolerate this mistreatment. A sense of liberation washed over me as I wrote my resignation letter. I knew I had to make a change, not just for myself but also for my family.

I sat down with my family, apologized, and promised to rebalance my life. I took time to self-reflect and identify how I got into this situation. The experience taught me to value myself and the critical lesson that no person or job was worth sacrificing my mental health or the well-being of my loved ones.

V. Self-Reflection and Realization

After I left my high-powered job in corporate America, I felt an unfamiliar mix of relief and uncertainty. My identity had been intertwined with my role as Chief Human Resources Officer at a major corporation for years. The toxic environment, exacerbated by the constant harassment from the execs, had driven me to the brink. But now, I am free.

I reflected on my strengths, likes, triggers, weaknesses, motivators, etc. As I identified and reconnected with who I am, I honed in on my expertise and a knack for *HR & Leadership Excellence*. I used the stress and conflict of my situation as FIRE and launched my consulting firm to help organizations understand how they need to treat their employees. Improper actions by employers create a risk for the organization and can be costly. Organizations must ensure that the leaders in position understand how to lead and the power of their influence.

After my resignation, I spent time with my family, reflecting on my professional journey. While I was passionate about HR and helping others, I realized that the traditional corporate environment wasn't conducive to my well-being. And let's just keep it real…I did not want to work for anyone again! One evening, while discussing my future with my husband, he suggested, "Why not start your own consulting firm? You have talked about it, have the experience, and are great at what you do."

The idea sparked a newfound excitement in me. I spent the next few days planning, networking, and setting up the foundation for my consulting firm, "Canary HR Consulting." My vision was clear: to help companies foster respect, maximize their talent, and minimize their risk.

Starting a business from scratch was daunting, but it wasn't my first time, and my determination outweighed my fears. I contacted old colleagues, attended industry events, and leveraged social media to build my brand. The firm began to gain traction, securing small projects that kept me busy and continued building my reputation.

The turning point came when an email landed in my inbox from an unexpected source. It was a former colleague from my old corporation. The company of the board he chaired was experiencing organizational changes and facing challenges with employee morale and retention. The former colleague and I worked closely together on HR issues, and he believed Canary HR could bring the change this organization needed.

I scheduled a meeting with the CEO and presented a comprehensive plan to transform the corporate culture. I proposed initiatives for leadership training, employee engagement programs, diversity and inclusion efforts, and a robust feedback system.

The CEO was impressed with my expertise and vision and decided to give me a chance. The organization awarded Canary HR a substantial contract, making it my first major client. Over the next few months, I worked tirelessly, implementing the proposed changes and seeing tangible results. Employee satisfaction improved, turnover rates decreased, and the overall atmosphere became more positive and productive.

The success of this contract attracted attention from other companies, leading to more opportunities for my firm. Canary HR started growing rapidly, but I carefully maintained a healthy work-life balance. I ensured my team worked reasonable hours, offered flexible schedules, and promoted a supportive environment.

My journey from a high-stress corporate job to becoming a successful business owner was arduous but fulfilling. I had transformed my pain into a purpose, helping companies build humane workplaces where employees could thrive. My story inspired countless others facing similar struggles, proving that with courage, self-leadership, and resilience, one could overcome adversity and FLOURISH.

VI. Implementing Change

My journey from corporate America to creating my consulting firm, Canary HR Consulting, was not just about professional change but also personal growth, self-care, and achieving a balanced life. By implementing these changes and prioritizing my personal growth and self-care, I transformed my life and set an example for others. My story became a testament to the power of resilience, balance, and the pursuit of Flourishing. The journey of implementing change starts with The Art of Self Leadership.

Implementing change through The Art of Self Leadership is a dynamic journey that requires continuous effort, reflection, and adjustment. By staying committed and adaptable, you can use the 8 steps to The Art of Self Leadership to effectively lead yourself toward meaningful and lasting change.

The 8 Steps to the Art of Self-Leadership:

1. Self-Awareness
   a. Identify Strengths and Weaknesses
   b. Reflect on personal and professional traits.

    c.   Acknowledge areas for improvement and potent skills.

    d.   Set Realistic Goals

        i.   Define clear, achievable objectives.

       ii.   Prioritize goals based on impact and feasibility.

2. Vision and Planning
   a. Develop a Vision
   b. Create a clear picture of the desired change.
   c. Ensure the vision aligns with personal values and long-term objectives.
   d. Create a Plan
      i. Outline actionable steps to achieve the vision.
      ii. Set milestones and timelines for assessing progress.

3. Commitment and Discipline
   a. Stay Committed
   b. Remind yourself of the purpose and benefits of the change.
   c. Stay resilient in the face of setbacks.
   d. Build Discipline
      i. Establish routines that support the change.
      ii. Practice consistent habits that align with goals.

4. Self-Motivation
   a. Cultivate Intrinsic Motivation
   b. Find internal reasons to motivate change.
   c. Reward yourself for small victories and progress.
   d. Use Positive Affirmations
      i. Practice self-encouragement and positive thinking.
      ii. Visualize success and the journey towards it.

5. Adaptability and Learning
   a. Embrace Flexibility
   b. Be open to adjusting plans as needed.
   c. Adapt strategies based on new insights or challenges.
   d. Continuous Learning
      i. Seek knowledge and skills necessary for change.
      ii. Leverage resources such as books, courses, and mentors.

6. Accountability
   a. Monitor Progress
   b. Regularly review and evaluate progress against set milestones.
   c. Adjust actions based on feedback and results.

d. Seek Feedback
    i. Welcome constructive criticism from peers, mentors, or coaches.
    ii. Use feedback to refine strategies and improve.

7. Reflect and Adjust
    a. Reflect Regularly
    b. Take time to reflect on what's working and what's not.
    c. Understand the root cause of any obstacles faced.
    d. Adjust Accordingly
        i. Modify actions and strategies based on reflection.
        ii. Continuously improve the approach towards the vision.

8. Sustain and Celebrate
    a. Sustain Change
    b. Integrate successful changes into daily routines.
    c. Maintain the mindset and habits that support continued growth.
    d. Celebrate Success
        i. Acknowledge and celebrate milestones and accomplishments.
        ii. Reflect on the journey and the evolution of self-leadership.

VII. Flourishing and Triumph

I prioritized myself for the first time. I reconnected with old hobbies and forged friendships based on mutual respect. I learned to say no and accepted that I couldn't please everyone—and that was okay.

My transition from a successful corporate career to founding my own consulting firm, Canary HR Consulting, began a transformative journey. Through strategic vision, relentless determination, and genuine empathy, I flourished in my career and created a lasting impact.

I believe in nurturing talent within my firm. I invest in my team's development, providing mentorship, training, and growth opportunities. This creates a motivated and skilled workforce and ensures the firm's sustainability and success.

My story and achievements inspired many aspiring HR professionals and entrepreneurs. My journey was a beacon of what could be achieved with passion, resilience, and a people-centric approach. My excellence did not go unrecognized. I received several awards acknowledging my contributions to business, HR, leadership, and community service. These accolades further cemented my position as a leader in my field. I received an Honorary Doctor of Philosophy for Business and the Presidential Lifetime Achievement Award.

VIII. From the Fire to Flourish

My career soared as I embraced roles that aligned with my values. Recognitions now felt earned, not burdened with doubt. Outside work, I led community initiatives, inspiring others with my story. I mentored young professionals, advocating for authenticity, self-leadership, and self-worth.

Reflecting on my journey, I felt gratitude for the lessons learned through adversity. I understood that rejection had shaped me, but it didn't define me. My story became a beacon of hope, teaching others that true triumph lies in embracing and flourishing as one's authentic self.

My self-leadership journey, from facing rejections in my early childhood to establishing my own successful firm and speaking on stages worldwide, offers valuable lessons that began with The Art of self-leadership.

Special Message

Hi there! Thank you for taking the time to read my journey. Remember, my path wasn't linear. Rejection doesn't define your journey, but how you respond does. By integrating self-leadership and maintaining a growth-centric mindset, you can transform setbacks into setups for future success, just like I did. It's your choice!

Are you ready to embrace self-leadership so you can Flourish in Business, Leadership, and Life?

Scan the QR code below and answer the questions to see where you are on the journey. You will also receive a free download: 8 Steps to Flourish from any rejection.

I look forward to supporting you as you transform from The Fire to Flourish!

DR. TANIA WHITE

Dr. Tania A. White is a wife and mother, published author, Lifetime Achievement Award-winning international keynoter, HR & Leadership Strategist, and coach. Dr. Tania is CEO of Canary HR Consulting, and I Flourish Leadership with nearly three decades of leadership experience in human resources and entrepreneurship. Tania has a deep-rooted passion for people, leadership, and excellence, which qualifies her to help people take their careers/businesses – and themselves – to unprecedented levels.

Dr. Tania's extensive business expertise has earned her invitations to speak on major corporate stages nationwide. Dr. Tania is an active member, volunteer, and leader with Delta Sigma Theta Sorority, Inc., and serves on numerous Boards and Committees. She is a Charter Member of Jack and Jill of America – Monarch Cities. She is a visionary leader who has significantly contributed to her community and the next generation. Her work has been featured on major media platforms such as ABC, NBC, FOX, CBS, talk shows, podcasts, leading newspapers, and magazines, including New York Weekly, alongside Tony Robbins and Les Brown.

Website: www.Iflourishleadership.com
Email: Tania@iflourishleadership.com
Instagram: https://www.instagram.com/drtaniawhite
LinkedIn: http://linkedin.com/in/taniawhite

Chapter Eleven

"WYNNING" IS ON THE OTHER SIDE OF FEAR!

MICHAEL D. WYNN

As a young boy, I once dreamed that life was as simple as sleeping, eating, going to school, playing, and growing up to become rich. Just like that! I didn't understand what it truly took to achieve wealth beyond my dreams and what I saw on TV. Despite my parents' financial struggles and our far-from-wealthy status, my mother instilled in me the motivation, vision, and creativity to envision future wealth. Even with little money, we lived with an "abundant thinking" mindset. My siblings and I were taught to focus on the abundance of what we had in terms of money, love, support, and possibilities rather than dwelling on what we lacked. Our faith, love, joy, relationships, spirit, and happiness gave us the best opportunities to feel rich, replacing any monetary figure for now.

As I grew into the man I am today, I had to make choices, search for and fix my mindset, and change to become a "Wynner" because of my birthright and connection with my family name. Our family reunion's signature logo, "Wynn-Winn," reflects our last name, W-y-n-n, passed down through generations. Despite occasional spelling errors that came during the years of slavery, turning it into W-i-n-n, the concept of being in a Wynn-Winn situation remains positive.

My journey began with my first business as a paperboy, earning recognition from the Michigan Press Association as an Outstanding Newspaper Boy. I didn't think much of it at the time. In my last year of high school, I had the opportunity to attend college, becoming the first of seven siblings to do so. I soon realized that business and accounting were the right majors for me. From my paperboy days through college, I developed a passion for understanding strategies to value, grow, and protect money. I dreamed of becoming a millionaire through a unique formula requiring multiple patents.

Throughout my career, I developed habits without realizing them, driven by a structured desire to achieve something. Early success allowed me to become a financial auditor, accountant, and tax preparer. However, I found that my own achievements brought fears that slowed me down. It felt like a dark side I didn't want to acknowledge. I believed I always had confidence until I faced obstacles. Instead of confronting them, I escaped into fantasy, dreaming of faraway places—this fear of winning led to excuses, a lack of motivation, and a trap of depression. Eventually, I was diagnosed with bipolar depression disorder.

Telling my story is difficult, but overcoming bipolar depression disorder requires confronting destructive thinking and unwanted behaviors stemming from fear. One of my biggest obstacles was feeling "crazy," but this was not me being part of a stigma or intending to offend anyone; it was just how I felt. However, I always share with my audience the incredible support I received from my therapist. She challenged me to understand the fears that held me back:

- **Fear of Failure:** This fear can prevent people from taking risks or pursuing new opportunities, stemming from a desire to avoid embarrassment, disappointment, or negative judgment. It keeps people within their comfort zones, avoiding challenges and missing out on growth and success.
- **Fear of Rejection:** This fear inhibits personal and professional relationships, often arising from past experiences or a need for acceptance and validation. It leads to reluctance to put oneself out there, limiting connections and opportunities.
- **Fear of the Unknown:** This fear causes people to avoid change and cling to the familiar, rooted in the discomfort of uncertainty. It can prevent individuals from exploring new paths, adapting to changes, or stepping outside their comfort zones, restricting their growth and adaptation.

Understanding and confronting your fears is crucial but not sufficient on its own. My journey toward success and well-being required persistence and repetition. When my therapist discussed habits with me, she highlighted some unique qualities I had yet to recognize as habits. At the time of my diagnosis, I had earned two financial certifications and was a licensed builder. My therapist pointed out that my achievements likely stemmed from habit formation. She recommended that I continue focusing on habits and recognize the importance of exercising positive affirmations, creating a positive environment, and challenging negative thoughts in my daily plan.

Exercising Positive Affirmations: Choose affirmations that resonate with you and your goals. For instance, statements like "I am capable of achieving my goals," "I am worthy of love and respect," or "Every day, I am becoming more confident and stronger." Repeat these affirmations daily, ideally in front of a mirror, to reinforce their positive impact. Over time, the benefits will include boosting your confidence and self-worth, reducing anxiety and stress by focusing on positive outcomes, and enhancing your overall mental well-being by fostering a positive self-image.

Creating a Positive Environment: Keep your physical living and working spaces clean, organized, and filled with things that bring you joy and inspiration. Surround yourself with supportive, positive people who uplift and encourage you, and limit time spent with those who drain your energy or bring negativity into your life. Engage in activities promoting happiness and relaxation, such as hobbies, exercise, and leisure time in nature. Over time, the benefits will include improved mental and emotional health, increased motivation and productivity, better stress management, and overall life satisfaction.

Challenging Negative Thoughts: Pay attention to your thoughts and recognize when they are negative or self-critical. Examine the evidence for and against these thoughts by asking yourself if they are based on facts or assumptions. Replace negative thoughts with more balanced and positive ones. For example, instead of thinking, "I always fail," reframe it to, "I may have failed this time, but I can learn from it and try again." Over time, the benefits will include reduced feelings of anxiety and depression, increased resilience and better coping skills, and improved overall mental health and quality of life.

By incorporating these practices into your daily life, you can significantly enhance your mental and emotional well-being, helping you to overcome fears and obstacles and move towards a more positive and fulfilling future.

With that advice, I quickly embraced researching habits and incorporating them into my daily life to become a true "Wynner." My goal was to build winning strategies with habits and share them with others, showing how to overcome obstacles with a repetitive formula I called the Habit Matrix. A habit is a goal to set, and goals are the results you want to achieve, but the system (my Habit Matrix) is the process that led me to the results I wanted to achieve. Your future is created by what you do today, not tomorrow, so winners must set winning goals. Elevate your success with clear goals and actions that produce desired results.

In my healing, I remembered a quote by Maya Angelou: "As soon as healing takes place, go out and heal somebody else." I felt obligated as a "Wynner" to speak about habits and share unique solutions that following habits can offer. As a financial expert with certifications in financial literacy training and fraud examination, I participated in community outreach programs to share life-changing financial habits. This is crucial because, in the U.S., less than 60% of Americans are financially literate, with Gen Z scoring even lower at 35-55% on a simple personal finance exam. I would discuss financial habits to consider:

- **Value Good Habits for Financial Stability:** Recognize the importance of stability in achieving financial goals without stress. This habit helps distinguish beneficial financial choices from detrimental ones, fostering a mindset prioritizing stability over immediate financial freedom. My eagerness to be financially free before being stable taught me the value of a habit matrix for financial stability.

- **Focus on Understanding:** Gaining understanding is crucial, especially in budgeting for personal and business finances. Cultivate a lifestyle of saving more than spending, handling debt responsibly, and understanding various debt types like student loans and credit card debt. Understanding your credit report is akin to an integrity report, revealing much about you. Investing and saving with a purpose in mind means teaching generational wealth management and passing it on. A habit matrix system will help you focus on understanding.
- **Keep It, It's Yours:** Know the importance of risk management and financial risks that can affect your personal and business life, such as job loss, unexpected penalties, investment loss, or fraud. Safeguarding finances is crucial, especially in the era of AI technology, where cybercrimes pose significant threats. A habit matrix system will help you keep what's rightfully yours.

Developing a habit formation system, like the one I discussed during my outreach, is vital. My call to action is for you to identify a habit strategy that positions you for success. Winners plan for big wins, like landing a desired job or achieving a dream career. I found it essential to follow five habit strategies for winning:

1. **Set Clear Goals:** By defining specific goals instead of vague objectives like "get fit," aim for specifics such as "lose 10 pounds in three months." Make them measurable to ensure your goals have measurable outcomes so you can track progress. For example, "increase sales by 20% in six months." They should be achievable by setting realistic goals that are challenging but attainable. Consider your current resources and constraints. Relevant goals should align with your broader life or business objectives, ensuring they are meaningful and worthwhile. Then make sure a time-stamp is attached as a deadline to your goals to create a sense of urgency and focus. For example, "complete the project by the end of Q2."
2. **Practice Self-Discipline:** To stay focused, concentrate on tasks that directly contribute to your goals, avoiding distractions like social media or unnecessary meetings. Create a routine establishing daily habits and schedules to maintain

consistency. This could include morning routines or designated work periods. Set boundaries to clearly define what is acceptable and unacceptable in your behavior and interactions to maintain discipline. Use tools to leverage productivity tools like calendars, to-do lists, and time management apps to stay organized and on track.

3. **Be Persistent and Repetitious:** Embrace challenges and view obstacles as opportunities to learn and grow. Develop a problem-solving mindset. Practice consistency regularly, review and adjust your plans as necessary, but remain committed to your long-term goals. Learn from failure by analyzing your setbacks to understand what went wrong and how you can improve. Use failures as stepping stones to success. Stay motivated by remembering your end goals and reminding yourself why you started. Surround yourself with supportive people who encourage your persistence.

4. **Prioritize Your Health and Well-Being:** Take on regular exercises to engage in physical activities like jogging, yoga, or strength training to maintain physical health and reduce stress. Eat a balanced diet rich in fruits, vegetables, lean proteins, and whole grains. Avoid excessive sugar and processed foods. Ensure you get 7-9 hours of sleep per night to allow your body and mind to recover and function optimally. Practice mindfulness, meditation, or other stress-reducing techniques to maintain mental well-being. Seek professional help if needed. "True wealth is having your health and knowledge of self" ~ Benjamin Franklin.

5. **Celebrate Small Wins and Tiny Breakthroughs:** Acknowledge your progress and recognize and appreciate each step you take toward your goal, no matter how small. Reward yourself by treating yourself when you reach milestones. This could be something simple like a favorite treat or a break from work. Stay positive and focus on what you've accomplished rather than what's left to do. This positive reinforcement builds momentum. Reflect on your success and achievements, and understand what contributed to your success, reinforcing positive behaviors.

I am deeply honored to have discovered that my "Wynning" is more powerful than the fears that once defined me. My journey was far from straightforward, and the path to becoming a "Wynner" was filled with numerous obstacles and significant moments. However, I am grateful for the opportunity to share some insights and strategies that may benefit you on your own journey.

> "The Challenge … Let others lead small lives, but not you. Let others argue over small things, but not you. Let others cry over small hurts, but not you. Let others leave their future in someone else's hands, but not you."
>
> ~ Jim Rohn

Here is what I ask of you: After reading this chapter, open your mind to positive thoughts and intentions on how habits can create life-changing events despite your challenges. Celebrate the victories you achieve, and feel free to contact me at the links below for motivational support as you shift into a persistent way of winning.

MICHAEL D. WYNN

Michael D. Wynn, aka "Coach Win," is a sought-after speaker, habit success strategist, financial expert, and best-selling author. Michael's diverse experiences motivated him to become certified as a financial literacy trainer, fraud examiner, and authenticity coach to empower individuals to be accountable and consistent with their habits.

Michael is known for his ability to connect with leaders, business teams, and organizations that are committed to a winning strategy through repetition and growth development. His leadership is distinguished by the creation of a tailored Habit Matrix, a tool that has proven to be highly effective in driving success. His authentic, motivational approach is underscored by the belief that 'Your Habits Will Determine Your Level of Success.' He is also the author of two bestselling books, "Habits Don't Lie" and "The Habit Effect."

Committed to raising financial literacy awareness, Michael was recognized with accolades such as the 2024 Lifetime Achievement Award from the Office of the President of the United States and the 2006 Outstanding Financial Literacy Award from the Michigan Accounting Aid Society.

Website:	https://www.coachwin.com
Email:	http://www.mikewynn@coachwin.com
Facebook:	https:// www.facebook.com/mikewynnhabits
Instagram:	https://www.instagram.com/mikewynnhabits
LinkedIn:	https://www.linkedin.com/in/michael-wynn-53348615/

THANK YOU

Thank you for reading Stories of the World's Greatest Speakers, Volume II.

Leave us a review by visiting us on Facebook at the Leadership Experience Tour, or by sending an email to info@fairconsultingroup.com.

Need Additional Leadership Mentoring or Coaching:

Shawn Fair is the founder of the Leadership Experience Tour. The #1 platform of its kind for aspiring speakers in the United States. He has trained over 300,000 leaders in the United States and abroad. His comprehensive and firsthand experience in the corporate world allows him to become an efficient trainer for companies and individuals.

The Leadership Experience Tour is a global platform designed to enhance the reach and visibility of new, emerging, and established speakers. We offer the resources, tools, and supportive services needed to succeed

To find out about programs and events visit:
https://leadershipexperiencetour.com